SEVEN
DAILY SINS

How the Gospel Redeems
Our Deepest Desires

GREED ENVY
SLOTH
PRIDE
LUST
GLUTTONY
WRATH

Jared C. Wilson

Published by LifeWay Press®
© 2012 Jared C. Wilson, Second Printing October 2012

No part of this work may be reproduced or transmitted in any form or by any means, electronic or mechanical, including photocopying and recording, or by any information storage or retrieval system, except as may be expressly permitted in writing by the publisher. Requests for permission should be addressed in writing to LifeWay Press®, One LifeWay Plaza, Nashville, TN 37234-0175.

ISBN: 978-1-4158-7241-3
Item: 005474747

Dewey Decimal Classification Number: 241.3
Subject Heading: SIN \ CHRISTIAN LIFE \ REPENTANCE

Printed in the United States of America.

Leadership and Adult Publishing
LifeWay Church Resources
One LifeWay Plaza
Nashville, Tennessee 37234-0175

We believe the Bible has God for its author; salvation for its end; and truth, without any mixture of error, for its matter and that all Scripture is totally true and trustworthy. The 2000 statement of *The Baptist Faith and Message* is our doctrinal guideline.

Unless otherwise noted, all Scripture quotations are taken from the Holman Christian Standard Bible®, copyright © 1999, 2000, 2002, 2003, 2009 by Holman Bible Publishers. Used by permission. Holman Christian Standard Bible®, Holman CSB®, and HCSB® are trademarks of Holman Bible Publishers.

Cover design by Leigh Ann Dans.

TABLE OF CONTENTS

ICON LEGEND

 Things to listen to

 Things to watch

 Expanding on biblical concepts

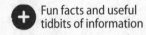 Fun facts and useful tidbits of information

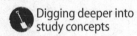 Digging deeper into study concepts

 Available tools for group leaders

 On the Web

MEET THE AUTHOR
JARED C. WILSON

Warning: Don't read this if you're not prepared to hear from a guy who wrote about gluttony while eating a cinnamon roll and who procrastinated writing a chapter on sloth. But if you want to study sin from an expert—I'm your man.

What I've learned from years of sinning is that it doesn't take much effort at all. I'm thankful that God's mercies are new every morning, because I wake up ready to disobey. That's how I roll. But in grace, God rolls out forgiveness in Christ abundant and free.

I've also learned how the gospel helps me see my sin, stop my sin, and starve my sin. Together, I hope we can learn more about this.

My name is Jared Wilson, and I'm a husband, dad, pastor, and writer. I'm amazed at how quickly I can mess up each of those roles simply by doing the wrong thing. But I'm even more amazed at how I manage to mess them up trying to do the right things under my own power and for the wrong reasons.

Again, don't read this book if you don't want to hear from an expert sinner. But if you're interested in hearing the inside scoop on grace-driven repentance and obedience, I'll be your huckleberry.

My friends in recovery programs remind me that every AA share time begins with an honest admission of failure: "My name is Joe, and I'm an alcoholic." The group then responds with, "Hi, Joe." This is not formulaic. It's redemptive. Joe has admitted he's a failure, and the response is not shame, condemnation, or nagging—it's welcome. The gospel is a welcome to failures, and *only* failures.

So, my name is Jared, and I'm a sinner. (I hope you like my study.)

DEADLY AND DAILY

Moving sin from "out there" to "in here"

GREED ENVY
SLOTH
PRIDE
LUST
GLUTTON
WRATH

Have you ever noticed how many lists are in the Bible? The writers of Scripture (and the Author inspiring them) seem to love lists. We get lists of names, lists of places, lists of measurements, lists of things to do, and lists of things not to do.

God knows we like bullet points. Having been a blogger for (nerd alert!) 10 years, I've discovered that my most popular blog posts are ones that include numbered lists.

Why?

We love lists because we like to compartmentalize. A list says: Here are the main points; now take action. When my wife sends me to the grocery store, she doesn't send me with an essay on why Downy fabric softener is better than Snuggle. She simply writes down "fabric softener." The grocery list is designed to be concise, clear, and easily actionable.

DOING AND BEING

We run into a problem with some of the lists in the Bible, particularly when we try to make them actionable. For example, look at what Paul wrote in Galatians 5:19-21:

> **"Now the works of the flesh are obvious: sexual immorality, moral impurity, promiscuity, idolatry, sorcery, hatreds, strife, jealousy, outbursts of anger, selfish ambitions, dissensions, factions, envy, drunkenness, carousing, and anything similar. I tell you about these things in advance—as I told you before—that those who practice such things will not inherit the kingdom of God."**

I don't know about you, but this list scares the living daylights out of me. The sorcery stuff I feel pretty safe on. But moral impurity? Outbursts of anger? Envy? And just in case you think you've found a loophole, Paul closed it up by forbidding "anything similar."

Paul's list is concise and clear. It says: Don't do these things if you want to inherit the kingdom of God. But it's not easily actionable. How do you stop sinning? Ever tried to just stop being jealous? How did that work out for you?

This list is important; it's Scripture. But apart from the context of the rest of Galatians, it can be despair-inducing. Thankfully, Paul offered another list shortly after the first:

> **"But the fruit of the Spirit is love, joy, peace, patience, kindness, goodness, faith, gentleness, self-control" (Galatians 5:22-23a).**

The most important thing I notice about this list is that it doesn't emphasize actions. It emphasizes qualities. The first list shows us things to do (or not do); this list shows us that the antidote to our sin—to the bad things we do—is good things we can be.

This is the most important lesson in the Christian's handling of sin: for the believer to "have crucified the flesh with its passions and desires" (Galatians 5:24), we must get beneath the surface of "dos and don'ts" and get right to those passions and desires. This means hearing and understanding the Bible's teaching on what sin is and where it comes from. Trying to remedy sin as we would complete a to-do list amounts to merely managing sin, not killing it. It's like mowing over the weeds in the yard rather than rooting them out.

TRYING TO REMEDY SIN AS WE WOULD COMPLETE A TO-DO LIST AMOUNTS TO MERELY MANAGING SIN, NOT KILLING IT.

INSIDE AND OUTSIDE

Jesus highlighted this change of perspective in response to the Pharisees' complaints that His disciples didn't wash their hands before eating (Matthew 15:2). The Pharisees weren't concerned about hygiene. They were worried about the "traditions of the elders," which was a concern for ritual cleanliness. For the Pharisees, this was a concern about the appearance of religious propriety—about obeying rules.

But for Jesus, "doing the right things" doesn't make somebody a right person. Obeying rules doesn't get rid of sin. So the practice of washing hands, in His theology, doesn't give somebody a clean heart.

Jesus said in Matthew 15:11:

> **"It's not what goes into the mouth that defiles a man, but what comes out of the mouth, this defiles a man."**

Jesus relocated the source of uncleanness from "out there" to "in here." The truth is that you don't become sinful through outside influences. You don't catch sin as you do a cold. You carry it around with you.

I once had a young lady tell me she wished she could get away from the negative influences and sinful temptations in our culture by moving to a deserted island all by herself. I told her not to go because she'd mess it up.

There are plenty of temptations in the world and lots of sins to be discovered, but the reason these are so dangerous is located right here in our own hearts. We can put as much sanitizer on our hands as we like, but we all carry the virus inside. That's why Jesus called

IF YOU'RE A GENUINE FOLLOWER OF JESUS, YOU'RE GENUINELY CONCERNED ABOUT YOUR SIN.

the Pharisees "whitewashed tombs" (Matthew 23:27)—because they looked great on the outside, but on the inside they were putrid, rotting death.

And this is why Jesus constantly relocated the source of goodness away from things to do and toward things to be. See, for instance, how the Beatitudes precede the practical matters of the Sermon on the Mount. And hear His words in Matthew 7:17:

> **"In the same way, every good tree produces good fruit, but a bad tree produces bad fruit."**

We must get at the root of our trees. If we want to produce good outer fruit for the kingdom of God, we must address our bad inner condition. And only the gospel of Jesus Christ has the power to do that.

DEADLY AND DAILY

One list we don't find in the pages of Scripture is what has traditionally been called "The Seven Deadly Sins." Historically attributed to Pope Gregory at the end of the sixth century, this categorization of the worst of "don'ts" has captured our creative imagination ever since. From Chaucer's *Canterbury Tales* and Dante's *Inferno* to Brad Pitt's *Se7en*, the Seven Deadly Sins—pride, lust, gluttony, greed, envy, sloth, and wrath—have become our culture's most commonly accepted definitive list of bad behaviors.

If you're a genuine follower of Jesus, you're genuinely concerned about your sin. You've discovered you can't stop sinning altogether, and apart from the power of God, there are specific areas of sin in your life you can't seem to kill—but you know you ought to, and you want to. You've likely learned that even when you stop doing bad things, you have trouble squelching bad thoughts or impure motives.

Here's the bad news: We all carry these Seven Deadly Sins in our hearts 24 hours a day. They're always lurking in us. That's why I've called this study Seven *Daily* Sins. We must be clear about what sin really is and where it comes from if we truly desire to crucify it.

Here's the good news: While our running the performance treadmill of moralism and our attempts at behavior management don't work, the power of Christ's perfect obedience, sinless sacrifice, and glorified resurrection do. And in Jesus and the power of His Spirit we find the freedom to confidently diagnose the root of our sins, boldly kill those sins through gospel-fueled repentance, and joyfully walk in newness of life.

That's what *Seven Daily Sins* is all about.

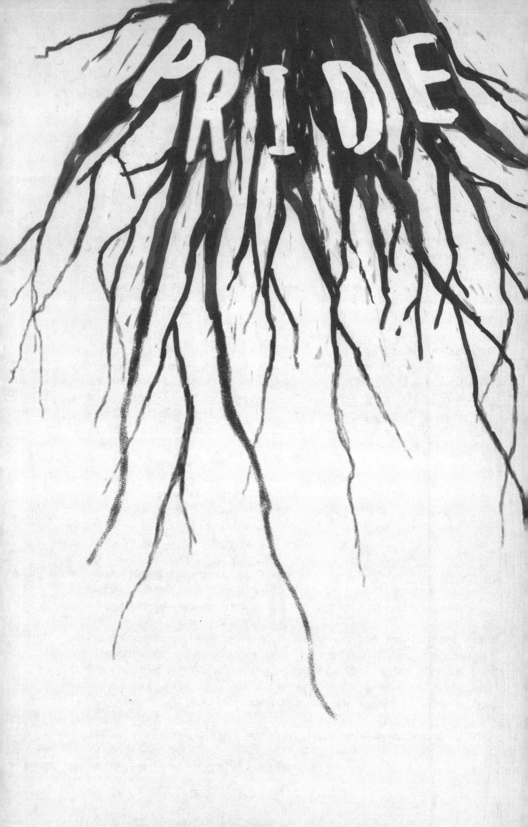

SESSION ONE

"'No! You will not die,' the serpent said to the woman. 'In fact, God knows that when you eat it your eyes will be opened and you will be like God, knowing good and evil.' Then the woman saw that the tree was good for food and delightful to look at, and that it was desirable for obtaining wisdom. So she took some of its fruit and ate it; she also gave some to her husband, who was with her, and he ate it" (Genesis 3:4-6).

Deep down in the recesses of every human soul is a cloying, ravenous monster ruthless for its own glory. This monster constantly clambers out of its dark pit, hunting and gathering food and trinkets—even collecting feelings and experiences. It's especially hungry for adulation and affirmation, but it's never satisfied. Its stomach is always grumbling for more.

This monster is us. Rather, it's the sinful nature in us. Paul described how this monster competes with our other inner desire—to love and obey God—this way:

> **"For in my inner self I joyfully agree with God's law. But I see a different law in the parts of my body, waging war against the law of my mind and taking me prisoner to the law of sin in the parts of my body. What a wretched man I am! Who will rescue me from this dying body?"** (Romans 7:22-24).

"This dying body" is at constant war with our freedom in Christ. This is why Jesus said we must crucify our sin monster every day:

> **"If anyone wants to come with Me, he must deny himself, take up his cross daily, and follow Me"** (Luke 9:23).

This monster does have a name, by the way. It's called Pride.

Deep down, every one of us harbors pride, and feeding the Pride Monster is often our greatest passion. That's why so many industries today are anchored on appeasing our pride—cosmetics, cosmetic surgery, exercise machines, designer clothes, protein shakes, hair replacement, and much more. Entire stores are filled with products designed to make us feel like we really are special.

Supply is high because demand is higher.

Can we benefit from these industries in a way that isn't prideful?

On magazine racks of grocery stores we now find titles like *All You* and *Self*, no longer bothering to veil attempts at the subject we're most interested in. (I sometimes joke with a friend who subscribes to these titles that we should start a magazine called *Others*. But we know it wouldn't sell.)

 Look up comedian Brian Regan's "me monster" routine online.

Because we're all, by default, conspicuous consumers, consumer culture is based on our firm belief that we're the sun around which everything orbits. A cable company giant even has an ad campaign assuring customers that they're "the center of the universe."

This is all blasphemy. Like Leo in *Titanic*, we stand at the bow, spreading our arms to span the horizon, not realizing we're headed for disaster. We proclaim, "I'm the king of the world!"

Then the ship sinks.

But it doesn't have to be this way.

TOOTING OUR OWN HORN

In *The Silmarillion*, the "prequel" of sorts to the classic trilogy *The Lord of the Rings*, author J. R. R. Tolkien crafts a parallel account to the creation of the world. Eru is the great creator of Middle Earth, but before time began he created the Ainur (a legion of angels or spirits) to reflect his own thoughts. Eru taught the Ainur to play a great musical composition. Together the music they played was powerful and majestic, and it reflected Eru's glory. But one of the Ainur named Melkor, whom Eru had especially gifted with knowledge and power, departed from the symphony to create his own song. The result was dissonance.

With this story, Tolkien illustrated how pride is fundamentally a rebellion against God's plan; it's indulging our desire to "toot our own horn." Tolkien played off the traditional account of the fall of Satan, of course, but he provided a powerful image of the way fallen mankind attempts to steal God's glory.

God created all of us with the capacity to worship. We're never not worshiping. Before the fall, Adam and Eve worshiped God only. But when they willfully succumbed to the serpent's temptation to "be like God" (Genesis 3:5), the wires of worship got crossed. They placed themselves on the thrones of their hearts. And ever since, while God's Word and His creation are declaring His glory, we depart from the song to sing about ourselves.

The Pride Monster devours everything in its path, seeking its own satisfaction, its own centrality, and therefore its own glory.

We see this in everything from the nagging desire to "keep up with the Joneses" to the propensity to become a "me monster" in social situations. It comes out even in passive aggression and manipulative silence. You don't have to be a loud and obnoxious braggart to be prideful; you can also withhold affection or service. Sometimes pride looks like sullen retreat, selfish solitude, or quiet judgmentalism. Sometimes we toot our own horns in the privacy of our own thoughts.

PRIDE'S DISASTROUS DESIRES

Pride is in the DNA of every other sin. Pride is essentially self-worship, and since all sin is failure to glorify God, pride is therefore the root sin from which all other sins come.

Think about it:

- Lust is rooted in self-gratification.
- Gluttony is rooted in self-satisfaction.
- Greed is rooted in self-love.
- Envy is rooted in self-honor.
- Sloth is rooted in self-justification.
- Wrath is rooted in self-exaltation.

So, if pride is in the DNA of the remaining "deadly sins," what's in the DNA of pride? We can make some deductions based on the moment of original sin. Here's the catastrophic event described in Genesis 3:1-6:

> "Now the serpent was the most cunning of all the wild animals that the LORD God had made. He said to the woman, 'Did God really say, "You can't eat from any tree in the garden"?'
>
> "The woman said to the serpent, 'We may eat the fruit from the trees in the garden. But about the fruit of the tree in the middle of the garden, God said, "You must not eat it or touch it, or you will die."'
>
> "'No! You will not die,' the serpent said to the woman. 'In fact, God knows that when you eat it your eyes will be opened and you will be like God, knowing good and evil.' Then the woman saw that the tree was good for food and delightful to look at, and that it was desirable for obtaining wisdom. So she took some of its fruit and ate it; she also gave some to her husband, who was with her, and he ate it."

Notice that pride is a response to a lie. The first thing out of the serpent's mouth was, "Did God really say...?" Already, the precursor to pride was a false belief about God and His Word.

Eve was savvy enough to reject this falsehood, but she wasn't faithful enough to reject the serpent's rebuttal. "You will be like God," he promised. This proved too much; the temptation too great. Eve opted to disbelieve God's promise and to disobey. She chose to believe in herself.

 To dig deeper into the first chapters of Genesis, check out *Creation Unraveled*, by Matt Carter and Halim Suh. Available for purchase at *threadsmedia.com*.

In short, behavior problems are belief problems. This is a really important point to remember, and it's something I'm going to revisit in each session because it will help us get to the root of our sins—not just manage the fruit of them.

The cause of Eve's disobedience was a three-pronged appeal that latched into her heart like a grappling hook:

- It was satisfying.
- It was pretty.
- It was enlightening.

Aren't these the very promises that still feed the Pride Monster inside of us? When we disobey God, it's invariably because we believe that something will satisfy more than He does; that something is more beautiful than He is; and that whatever this something is, it's something we deserve—because we hold the rank of lord, just like God does.

The sin of pride is attempting to thieve from God's glory as if it belonged to us. It's an attempt at mutiny. The three-pronged temptation of the forbidden fruit said to Eve, "You can be a god like God," which was just a subtle way of saying, "You can be a god *instead* of God." When we disobey any of God's commands, we're saying essentially the same thing: "God, You're not God. I am."

The problem is, when we place ourselves at the center of the universe, everything goes wrong. The result of Adam and Eve's disobedience was creation gone haywire. God laid a curse upon the rebels (Genesis 3:14-27), and to demonstrate just how devastating and far-reaching the sin of pride is, He also cursed creation itself.

What would happen if we were to knock the sun out of the center of our solar system? Chaos. Disaster. Death. Similarly, when we attempt to usurp God's rightful place at the center, pridefully living self-centered lives, the result is disastrous disorder. C. S. Lewis made this point when he wrote:

> "It is Pride which has been the chief cause of misery in every nation and every family since the world began. Other vices may sometimes bring people together: you may find good fellowship and jokes and friendliness among drunken people or unchaste people. But pride always means enmity—it is enmity."[1]

If you remember, *enmity* is the word God used in Genesis 3:15 to describe how disobeying Him affected the relationship between the serpent and the offspring of man. (The word is

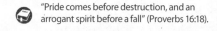

"Pride comes before destruction, and an arrogant spirit before a fall" (Proverbs 16:18).

hostility in the *Holman Christian Standard Bible*.) But as we progress through the details of the curse, we see that the same enmity (hostility) extends to all relationships—Eve will usurp Adam's authority and Adam will domineer over Eve, for example. This demonstrates that pride isn't just disastrous for our right standing with God; it's disastrous for our relationships with others. Sin is fundamentally anti-social.

We see this effect in the pattern of the Ten Commandments. The First Commandment is:

"Do not have other gods besides Me" (Exodus 20:3).

Each of the remaining nine Commandments are violations of the First Commandment. If we make graven images to worship, it's because we have other gods before God, of course. But if we violate the command to honor the Sabbath or abuse God's name, we're also demonstrating disobedience to God's command to keep Him first as God.

When we get to the "horizontal" commands in the list (Commandments 5 through 10), they also help us to have no other gods before God. If I steal from you, after all, it's because I have the god of money or possessions or vengeance—because I have the god of myself—before the one true God. And the same goes if I murder or commit adultery and all the rest. Every sin is a violation of the First Commandment. And, therefore, every sin is fundamentally the sin of pride.

Think of the most recent conflict you've had with someone close to you—a friend, spouse, family member, coworker, roommate, and so on. How did pride (yours or theirs) contribute to the conflict?

How would you define worship? How is pride self-worship?

PRIDE DIAGNOSTICS
Read Isaiah 44:12-20.

This passage is a reflection on the foolishness of idolatry. Notice the seamless transition from the business of life to the worship of graven images. Workmen were making lumber, shaping iron, and drawing pictures. They were making fires, planting trees, and cooking food. Suddenly they were worshiping the products of their labors; they turned their work into idolatry. According to verses 19-20, they weren't even thinking.

 Watch the *Seven Daily Sins* video "Pride," available for purchase at *threadsmedia.com/sevendailysins*.

The way the idolaters moved from the daily business of life and work to sin illustrates how all sin is basically idolatry and how all idolatry is basically self-worship. There's just one step to prideful self-worship: exist. According to Isaiah 44:12-20, it's deceptively easy to worship ourselves as gods. All we have to do is mind our own business.

One of the key points in this passage (v. 19) is also about how blind we are to this sin. Self-centered people don't usually think of themselves as self-centered. So let's reflect. Let's ask some diagnostic questions of ourselves to see if, perhaps, we've set up some blind spots where our prideful self-interest lies.

1. When making your daily commute, do you often find yourself frustrated that everybody else is driving too slow or too fast? (Because you're the standard by which everyone should drive, right?)
2. Look over your last several social media updates. Do a large percentage of them complain about something?
3. Do you struggle often with impatience and short-temperedness?
4. Is it common for others to charge you with being too defensive?
5. Do you have a reputation for being thin-skinned or too sensitive?
6. Do you spend a lot of time worrying about what others think of you?
7. Do you not care what others think of you, so much so that it causes you to be un-gentle with people or insensitive to them?
8. Do you have trouble making friends, and is your understanding of this problem that there's something wrong with all of them?
9. Is it difficult for you to let it go when your accomplishments aren't recognized or you're not congratulated?
10. Do people close to you perceive you as either lazy or a workaholic?

These questions are admittedly subjective. It's possible, for instance, that a reputation for selfishness is undeserved. (It's not likely, but it's possible.) But maybe your answers to those questions have you feeling very proud of yourself. In that case: Gotcha!

According to the Bible, if we're breathing, we have pride deep down inside:

> **"We all went astray like sheep; we all have turned to our own way . . . "**
> **(Isaiah 53:6).**

> **" . . . there is no one who seeks God" (Romans 3:11).**

So here's one final diagnostic question to determine if pride is an issue for you:

11. Do you sin?

You may have answered "no" to diagnostic questions 1 through 10, but if you answered "yes" to number 11, you're now face to face with the biggest problem in your life: pride. (And if you think the answer to number 11 is "no," read 1 John 1:10 below.)

GETTING AT THE ROOT

The bad news about pride is that God is actively opposed to those who coddle and indulge it. Throughout the Scriptures, we find Him rebuking pride with vengeful foreboding and warning the proud about the wrath that's due them. Check out Proverbs 16:5, for instance:

> **"Everyone with a proud heart is detestable to the LORD; be assured, he will not go unpunished."**

What's the solution, then? How do we kill pride? Isaiah 44:20 points away from ourselves, saying this about self-worshipers:

> **"His deceived mind has led him astray, and he cannot deliver himself . . . "**

In his classic work *The Expulsive Power of a New Affection*, Thomas Chalmers expressed the problem this way:

> "The love of God and the love of the world are two affections not merely in a state of rivalship, but in a state of enmity—and that so irreconcilable that they cannot dwell together in the same bosom. We have already affirmed how impossible it were for the heart, by any innate elasticity of its own, to cast the world away from it, and thus reduce itself to a wilderness. The heart is not so constituted, and the only way to dispossess it of an old affection is by the expulsive power of a new one."[2]

Chalmers said what Isaiah 44:20 says. We need deliverance, but it's impossible for our prideful hearts to deliver themselves of pride by their own power.

We try, though, don't we? Have you ever simply tried to be less selfish? It may have worked in terms of your behavior—for a while. But managing selfish expressions can't kill prideful desires inside of us. We can't help but naturally and instinctively praise what we find interesting or lovely.

So, if we struggle to deflect our inner (or outer) praise away from ourselves to God, what does that say about what we think of God?

 "If we say, 'We don't have any sin,' we make Him a liar, and His word is not in us" (1 John 1:10).

What does the Bible say about the relationship between good works and salvation?

Do you remember the fantastic opening sequence of *Raiders of the Lost Ark*? Indiana Jones had journeyed deep into a cavern in the South American jungle. He reached the place where a shiny idol sat, perched on a weight-sensitive pedestal. Indy sized it up. He ran the guesstimated calculations in his head. He pulled out a pouch of sand, felt its weight in his hand, hoping it was equally heavy to the idol grinning back at him. He poured a bit out. He knew the only way to safely dispossess the pedestal of its old affection was the equal weight of a new one. He steeled himself. He stretched his arms. Quick as lightning, he snatched the idol from its stony cradle while simultaneously putting the sandbag in its place.

There was a pause. Nothing happened. He smiled, turned—and then chaos broke loose. Actually, the cave broke loose. A gigantic stone bowling ball came tumbling down. Poison darts started shooting out of the walls. Pits opened up. Walls slammed down. And before you knew it, Alfred Molina had a wall of spikes through his skull.

This is what happens when we try replacing an idol with religious behavior. We think it'll work. But it's just a bag of sand. We can't deliver ourselves. Instead, we need the power of a new affection for God to expel the old affection for ourselves. We need a power that will get right down to the root of our hearts, not just offer some tips for behavior modification.

But such a power can't come from us.

THE CURE FOR PRIDE

The power to expel pride from our hearts isn't in a set of advice, tips, or practical steps. Those things can be helpful in our efforts to worship God in our obedience, but they have no power of themselves. Instead, we find the power to expel pride in a story. (By "story," I don't mean that it's not true; I only mean to say that it's history, that it's something that already happened as opposed to something left to do.)

Here's a key part of that saving story:

> **"Then Jesus was led up by the Spirit into the wilderness to be tempted by the Devil. After He had fasted 40 days and 40 nights, He was hungry. Then the tempter approached Him and said, 'If you are the Son of God, tell these stones to become bread.' But he answered, 'It is written: Man must not live on bread alone but on every word that comes from the mouth of God.'**

Listen to "The War Inside" by Switchfoot from the *Seven Daily Sins* playlist, available at *threadsmedia.com/sevendailysins*.

"Then the Devil took Him to the holy city, had Him stand on the pinnacle of the temple, and said to Him, 'If you are the Son of God, throw Yourself down. For it is written: He will give His angels orders concerning you, and they will support you with their hands so that you will not strike your foot against a stone.'

"Jesus told him, 'It is also written: Do not test the Lord your God.' Again, the Devil took Him to a very high mountain and showed Him all the kingdoms of the world and their splendor. And he said to Him, 'I will give You all these things if You will fall down and worship me.' Then Jesus told him, 'Go away, Satan! For it is written: "Worship the Lord your God, and serve Him only."'

"Then the Devil left Him, and immediately angels came and began to serve Him" (Matthew 4:1-11).

Did you notice how the temptation of Jesus parallels the temptation of Adam and Eve? Those three desires showed up again. Satan told Jesus to turn the stones to bread, appealing to His appetite in the same way Eve saw the fruit was good for food. Satan told Jesus to employ His access to angels, appealing to His deity in a similar way that Eve was tempted to "be like God" (Genesis 3:5). Satan also showed Jesus the kingdoms of the world in all their glory, demonstrating their shiny appeal, echoing how Eve found the forbidden fruit "delightful to look at" (Genesis 3:6).

Notice also how Jesus' response to Satan mirrored Eve's initial response to the serpent. He quoted Scripture. Satan offered a detour from God's will, and the proper retort was, "It is written." But while Eve ran out of biblical ammunition to combat Satan's "Did God really say?", Jesus continued rebuking the Devil with what God really said.

That's a valuable lesson. Pride has us saying, "I am God." But the truth will set us free.

What this shows us is that total redemption is only available through Jesus' work, not ours. Where Adam and Eve (and we) messed up, Jesus came through. Where we fail, He succeeds. We're sinful through and through, so there's no sacrifice we can make that won't be tainted with our inability to perfectly withstand temptation. But as His temptation in the wilderness reveals, Jesus was sinless, and so His sacrifice was effective. Here, in a foreshadowing of the cross, Jesus redeemed Adam's and Eve's (and our) susceptibility to pride.

The real power to kill the Pride Monster, then, is not in our summoning up some inner religious strength or telling ourselves that we're good enough, smart enough, and that people like us.

 "The fact that Jesus had to die for me humbled me out of my pride. The fact that Jesus was glad to die for me assured me out of my fear."[3] —Timothy Keller

The real power to kill the Pride Monster is found in the good news that Jesus killed it through His sinless sacrifice on the cross.

In their book *Counsel from the Cross*, Elyse Fitzpatrick and Dennis Johnson wrote:

> "Most of us have never really understood that Christianity is not a self-help religion meant to enable moral people to become more moral. We don't need a self-help book; we need a Savior. We don't need to get our collective act together; we need death and resurrection and the life-transforming truths of the gospel."[4]

So how do we access this power? By beholding the glory of Jesus in the beautiful gospel. By meditating on the gospel, chewing on it, and stewing in it. By refusing to "graduate" from it. If we ever think the gospel is simply our "ticket to heaven," we immediately enter the danger zone of disobeying Galatians 3:3:

> **"Are you so foolish? After beginning with the Spirit, are you now going to be made complete by the flesh?"**

How would you answer those two questions?

In terms of your spiritual walk, what do you do well as a follower of Jesus? Where are you contributing to God's kingdom?

Where do you struggle in following the example set by Christ?

Check out 2 Corinthians 3:18:

> **"We all, with unveiled faces, are looking as in a mirror at the glory of the Lord and are being transformed into the same image from glory to glory; this is from the Lord who is the Spirit."**

It's in beholding Jesus as glorious that we're transformed into real reflections of His glory ourselves. There's no other way that isn't prideful.

Leading a group? Find extra questions and teaching tools in the leader kit, available for purchase at *threadsmedia.com/sevendailysins*.

THE CURE FOR ALL SIN

This is also the approach I plan to to take in the next six sessions. The way to repent of lust, gluttony, greed, envy, sloth, and wrath is by tasting and seeing how Jesus has conquered them in His life and death.

Do you remember the myth story we encountered earlier from Tolkien's *The Silmarillion*? The Ainur (angel) named Melkor departed from the creator's symphony to sing his own song, to "toot his own horn," and the result was discord and disharmony. His rebellion created an awful dissonance. The creator, Eru, forbade Melkor from singing his own song, but throughout the history of Middle Earth, Melkor kept trying, enlisting help from any who would choose evil. Eventually Eru put a final stop to Melkor's song, drowning the rebel out with a declaration of Eru's own glory and throwing Melkor, bound in chains, into a great void.

Here's what Eru (also called Ilúvatar) said to Melkor during the beginning moments of his rebellion:

> "Mighty are the Ainur, and mightiest among them is Melkor; but that he may know, and all the Ainur, that I am Ilúvatar, those things that ye have sung, I will show them forth, that ye may see what ye have done.

> And thou, Melkor, shalt see that no theme may be played that hath not its uttermost source in me, nor can any alter the music in my despite. For he that attempteth this shall prove but mine instrument in the devising of things more wonderful, which he himself hath not imagined."[5]

That's a reflection of what God has done in Christ. Satan continues to bait the beasts of pride in each of us—not that we need much help—and we all, in a variety of ways, sing our own praises. But God will have His own glory. He's a jealous God. So He sent His Son to proclaim the great song-story of the gospel, and, at the cross, He conquered sin and Satan "once for all" (Hebrews 7:27).

Conquering the Seven Deadly Sins, then, means conquering the first sin of pride. And conquering the first sin of pride means seeing Jesus, the glorious Savior, at the center of the universe. When we're prideful, we're attempting to elevate ourselves, to save ourselves. But the real way to be elevated is to be humbled (in Christ), and the real way to be saved is to die (with Christ).

I like the way Trevin Wax writes about this idea:

> "Ironically, when we live as if our personal story is at the center of our universe, we struggle to find meaning and significance. But when Christ is at the center

and we are pushed to the periphery, it is then—in that place of seeming obscurity and insignificance—that we find true worth and value, by giving glory to the crucified and risen King with whom we can become united through faith."[6]

We all must battle the deadly sin of pride daily. Let's make sure we're doing it with the only power the Bible prescribes: the gospel.

THROUGH THE WEEK

> **Watch:** If you have a couple hours to spare this week, gather some friends and watch the 2005 version of *Pride and Prejudice*. (If you really have some spare time, try powering through the BBC version from 1995.) Keep these two questions in mind as you watch:

1. What are the diffrent types of pride that show up in the story?
2. What are the consequences of pride in the characters' lives?

> **Memorize:** Read Romans 12:16 every day this week: "Be in agreement with one another. Do not be proud; instead, associate with the humble. Do not be wise in your own estimation." See if you can commit those words to memory by the end of the week.

> **Pray:** Whenever you pray over the next several days, ask the Holy Spirit to bless you with increased compassion, kindness, humility, gentleness, and patience (see Colossians 3:12).

NOTES

SESSION TWO

"You have heard that it was said, Do not commit adultery. But I tell you, everyone who looks at a woman to lust for her has already committed adultery with her in his heart. If your right eye causes you to sin, gouge it out and throw it away. For it is better that you lose one of the parts of your body than for your whole body to be thrown into hell. And if your right hand causes you to sin, cut it off and throw it away. For it is better that you lose one of the parts of your body than for your whole body to go into hell!" (Matthew 5:27-30).

John Calvin said that our hearts are idol factories. If that's true—and I think it is—we also have infernal little Research and Development departments in those factories working on new ways for us to worship the idols we produce.

Nowhere is this more evident than in the ever-innovative world of pornography. The makers of material specifically designed to incite and satisfy sexual lust are constantly searching for new ways to, pardon the pun, expose their wares to consumers. Some sociologists and technology gurus have even credited the pornography industry with driving the consumer branch of the technology industry in general—including this excerpt from an article in an influential journal:

> "Historically, the development of new media has been advanced by the creators of pornography. This was evident as communications media evolved from vernacular speech to movable type, to photography, to paperback books, to videotape, to cable and pay-TV, to 900 phone lines, to the French Minitel, and to the Internet. In short, pornography, far from being an evil that the First Amendment must endure, is a positive good that encourages experimentation with new technology. Accordingly, society should not view cyberpornographers as pariahs, rather they should be viewed as explorers who pave the roads for civilization to follow."[1]

Those poor, picked-on pornographers. What's wrong with us that we don't see them as heroes? The reality is that cyber-pornographers are only pioneers in the sense that Internet spammers are pioneers—successful at getting through any barriers in order to advertise their junk to susceptible people. Like spammers, pornographers aren't content to wait for consumers to seek out their products; they're finding increasingly new and bold ways to shove their products right under our noses.

The producers of pornography have capitalized on something insatiable in the human species, especially among males: lust. They've become the reigning masters of the mantra embraced everywhere from Park Avenue advertising firms to evangelical churches' provocative sermon series—namely, "sex sells."

And we're buying it like a teenage boy in a . . . well, in a porn shop. The pornographic appeal has become so ubiquitous that it has seeped from shady downtown theaters and seedy California studios into nearly every nook and cranny of mainstream life. The bottom line is that pornography isn't just for "those" perverts anymore. It's for all of us perverts, too.

And here's the worst part: Pornography is just one facet of that ever-adapting sin called lust.

 Among Internet users, 43 percent visit pornographic Web sites. Of these 40 million regular visitors, 33 percent are women.[2]

WHAT IS LUST?

According to the traditional Seven Deadly Sins, "lust" denotes an immoral sexual desire. And that qualifier "immoral" is important.

Once when I was an assistant in a church youth ministry, we took teenagers to the beach. While we were there, the youth pastor made it a rule that any guy caught looking at a girl in her swimsuit would have to do 20 push-ups. This approach, it was thought, would curb their lustfulness.

As I think back on this experiment, it occurs to me that if we really wanted to be that extreme about curbing lust, we wouldn't have taken teenage boys to the beach where girls in swimsuits would be frolicking in the first place! But it also occurs to me that this experiment, on the surface anyway, misunderstood what lust even is.

Is it lust for a man to notice that a woman is attractive? Is it lust for him to be sexually attracted to her—to feel a tug in her direction? (Or vice versa.) I don't believe so. And I think the church might be doing some damage to generations of young people by unintentionally shaping them to think of sexual desire as sinful or sexuality as ungodly.

The truth is that God has wired both men and women to find members of the opposite sex attractive. We were made to recognize beauty. Furthermore, the sex drive inside of us was put there by God. It's not a mistake, not a flaw in our design. The Christian thing to do, then, is not to train men and women to think of sexual attraction as sinful, but to train them to think about sexual attraction in a Christ-like manner.

Do you agree that someone can feel physically attracted to another person without also experiencing lust? Why or why not?

What would've been a better approach to helping young men on that beach curb lust than simply to command push-ups after every perceived look?

Lust is not sexual attraction. Lust isn't seeing a person or even noticing that someone is attractive. Lust is the immoral desire that attacks and infects our seeing and noticing—the "look after the look." What we do after we experience sexual attraction is the vital place of victory or defeat in the war against sin.

Lust may feel natural to many of us—an easy reaction to stimuli. But lust is never accidental. It's always intentional. This is how Jesus framed the point of lust:

> **"You have heard that it was said, Do not commit adultery. But I tell you, everyone who looks at a woman to lust for her has already committed adultery with her in his heart" (Matthew 5:27-28).**

Jesus emphasized the intentionality behind lust—the decision being made. Noticing a woman isn't sin. Looking at a woman isn't sin. Recognizing that a woman is attractive isn't sin. But looking at a woman "to lust" is a sin. (And, of course, this goes for women looking at men, too.) Lust is the intention to gratify immoral sexual desire.

This is clear because of where Jesus located the sin: "in his heart." If your head is turned by Megan Fox or Brad Pitt, it's not what you've done outwardly that defines it as a sin, but what you've done inwardly. After you turned your head, what happened inside of it? A mental undressing? Imagined sexual scenarios? A comparison between this vision and your spouse?

Now you're in the territory of lust. And no matter how quickly you got there, you got there on purpose.

Do you agree that lust is always intentional? Why or why not?

It's easy to pick on guys when it comes to lust and pornography, but what are some cultural evidences that women share in this struggle?

LUST DIAGNOSTICS
It's easy to become deceived by the sin of lust.

We may think that something so internal or private can't be dangerous, but this is just part of the package of lies we believe to maintain our habits unhindered. If you don't think lust is a big deal, it may be because you haven't done a lot of self-reflection on the matter.

Ask yourself these diagnostic questions. You don't have to write your answers down or share them with your group—unless your group is designed to be a safe place to confess sin and receive biblical counsel—but be brutally honest with yourself.

 "I have made a covenant with my eyes. How then could I look at a young woman?" (Job 31:1).

1. Do you specifically pick movies or TV shows to watch because you know there might be sexual content in them?
2. Do you struggle to concentrate in conversation with someone when an attractive member of the opposite sex walks by?
3. Do you view pornography?
4. Do you read romance novels or watch romantic movies and find yourself discouraged because it doesn't resemble your own romantic or sexual prospects?
5. If you're dating someone, is it "impossible" to be alone together without crossing lines physically?
6. If you're married, do you mentally compare your spouse's sexual attractiveness or sexual abilities to how you imagine others are?
7. Do you find it difficult to stop mentally undressing others? Do you put yourself in positions of opportunity to do so?
8. Do you "creep" others' photo albums on social networking sites, looking for sexually suggestive or attractive pictures?
9. Do you find that the majority of the compliments you give to others—male or female, whether you mean it sexually or not—involves their physical appearance?
10. Has anyone every confronted you for having wandering eyes?

If you answered yes to any one of those questions, especially number 3, it's an indication that you may have a problem with lust. If you answered yes to more than one of those questions, you definitely have a problem.

The good news is that help is available. The bad news is that help is not available through your effort alone. Dallas Willard wrote: "The fact is that people engaged with the use of pornography have decided to be there and have not decided not to be there. But 'will power' alone will not solve the problem."[3]

In order to solve the problem, we must first identify what the problem really is.

A CLOSER LOOK

A few years ago, the business world was contemplating the financial struggles of Hugh Hefner's Playboy enterprise. Apparently, the magazine that once set the pornographic standard was no longer raking in the dough. At first blush, many people found this news encouraging. It's good that *Playboy* magazine isn't lucrative, right? But the reality behind those financial struggles wasn't so exciting.

Playboy didn't lose revenue because people's taste for sexually explicit material had waned. *Playboy* lost revenue because people's tastes for sexually explicit material had become more intense, making *Playboy*'s visual offerings "tame" by comparison. People began to think: *Why pay six bucks for a magazine of merely nude women when images and videos of hardcore sex are available for free online?*

Again, that's just one indicator that the presence of sexual lust in our society is worse than ever. Other symptoms include a greater focus on sexuality in advertising, more explicit movies and TV shows, increases in adultery and premarital sex—not to mention things like "sexting," "swinging," and the continued horror of human trafficking. Look at all that, and one thing is clear: We're sick with this stuff (and getting sicker).

What are some signs that the lust problem is, culturally speaking, getting worse?

Did the lessons your church taught about lust as you were growing up prove helpful? Why or why not?

If you didn't grow up going to church, what advice, if any, did you receive from your parents or teachers about lust and handling sexual attraction?

What many who struggle with lust have discovered is that once you give it an inch, it will take you a hundred miles. What worked to gratify in the beginning stops working; the lustful consumer needs more of it, needs it to be more explicit, and needs it more often.

The Bible doesn't tiptoe around reality but speaks to this all-consuming hold in a blunt way. Authors write about being "captivated" (Proverbs 6:25) and "inflamed" (Ezekiel 16:30; Romans 1:27) by lust. Check out the words this father has for his son about the seduction of sexual immorality:

> **"Though the lips of the forbidden woman drip honey and her words are smoother than oil, in the end she's as bitter as wormwood and as sharp as a double-edged sword. Her feet go down to death; her steps head straight for Sheol" (Proverbs 5:3-5).**

Despite the attractive appeal of lust and all that it represents, giving in to sexual immorality is choosing death. Lust is a snare of our own making, but once we've caught ourselves, it takes a supernatural power to become free.

Watch the *Seven Daily Sins* video
"Lust," available for purchase at
threadsmedia.com/sevendailysins.

If you've ever been wrapped up in lustful compulsions or the habitual use of pornography—as I have—you know how difficult the process of quitting can be. Once gratified, guilt and shame set in. You vow never to indulge in that sin again, committing to try harder. But in moments of weakness and doubt, the appeal proves too strong. And the cycle repeats. The apostle Paul wrote about such inner spiritual warfare this way:

> "For I know that nothing good lives in me, that is, in my flesh. For the desire to do what is good is with me, but there is no ability to do it. For I do not do the good that I want to do, but I practice the evil that I do not want to do. Now if I do what I do not want, I am no longer the one doing it, but it is the sin that lives in me. So I discover this principle: When I want to do what is good, evil is with me. For in my inner self I joyfully agree with God's law. But I see a different law in the parts of my body, waging war against the law of my mind and taking me prisoner to the law of sin in the parts of my body" (Romans 7:18-23).

The good things Paul wanted to do, he couldn't do. The bad things he didn't want to do, he ended up doing. He felt taken prisoner. Sound familiar? There's a war being waged. Have you ever engaged in lust only to find yourself demoralized, disappointed, and degraded? You hear echoes of the famous words of Michael Corleone in *The Godfather: Part III*: "Every time I think I'm out, they pull me back in."

What emotions do you hear in Paul's words? What emotions do you experience when you read them?

Are you winning or losing the war against lust?

Here's the problem: *As long as we think of sin only as behavior, we'll be content with behavior modification.* But if we remember that sin isn't just about what we do, but about the condition of our hearts, we'll be able to combat it more fiercely. The first step to conquering lust is knowing the enemy well.

THE GRAPPLING HOOK

Let's take a deeper look at pornography for a moment. What makes it so powerful? How does it become such a perfect storm of sinful appeal? I believe it's because it combines a trifecta of worldly temptations.

Here's what the apostle John said are the things that "belong to the world":

> " ...the lust of the flesh, the lust of the eyes, and the pride in one's lifestyle—
> is not from the Father, but is from the world" (1 John 2:16).

This three-part temptation is the same temptation Eve found so undeniable in Genesis 3:6.

- *The lust of the flesh*: "Then the woman saw that the tree was good for food ..."
- *The lust of the eyes*: " ...and delightful to look at ..."
- *Pride in one's lifestyle*: " ...and that it was desirable for obtaining wisdom."

It's also clear that today's pornography contains the same DNA as that original temptation.

- *The lust of the flesh*: Pornography arouses our sexual desire and claims (falsely) to satisfy it.
- *The lust of the eyes*: Pornography sinks its hooks into our hearts through visual appeal.
- *Pride in one's lifestyle*: Because pornography is self-gratification, use of it is an act of pride. And because it requires more and more of it to gratify, like any drug promising a high, it encourages accumulation. There's also a "secret knowledge" factor for men especially—the sense of voyeurism, the solitary exulting in something illicit. It's like Tolkien's Gollum in his cave with his birthday present, a simultaneous celebration and corruption, a delight and degradation, an acquisition of esteem and power. But this is all just smoke and mirrors.

The three appeals of original sin are the three prongs of pornography's grappling hook, and they help explain how easy it is to get ensnared—and how difficult it is to escape.

But there's good news for those wrapped up in pornography or lust or any other sin. Jesus was tempted as we are, and He was perfectly obedient (Matthew 4:1-11). He resisted this same temptation by resisting the Devil in the desert, thereby redeeming our susceptibility, and He took our sin to the cross, thereby conquering sin on our behalf!

The bottom line is that Jesus conquered original sin; therefore, He conquered all that's in the world—including lust. And He can forgive you for and redeem you from lustful actions.

APPLYING THE GOSPEL TO LUST
In Matthew 5, after Jesus equated lust in our hearts with committing physical adultery (vv. 27-28), He offered this prescription for killing lust:

....

 Listen to "Killa" by Lecrae from the
Seven Daily Sins playlist, available at
threadsmedia.com/sevendailysins.

SESSION TWO SEVEN DAILY SINS

"If your right eye causes you to sin, gouge it out and throw it away. For it is better that you lose one of the parts of your body than for your whole body to be thrown into hell. And if your right hand causes you to sin, cut it off and throw it away. For it is better that you lose one of the parts of your body than for your whole body to go into hell!" (Matthew 5:29-30).

The stakes are high! This is why the Bible speaks radically about dealing with lust. The damage lust does to our hearts is massive, so our battle against it must be furious.

By refocusing the sin of adultery into our hearts, Jesus wasn't saying what we do with our bodies doesn't matter. He meant if we want to really honor God with obedience, we must identify where sin lives—not "out there," but "in here."

What do you think Jesus meant in Matthew 5:29-30 when He said to gouge out our eyes and cut off our hands?

It would be silly to believe Jesus is speaking about literally plucking out our eyes or lopping off our hands. So what is He saying? There's both a practical and spiritual application of Jesus' command.

First, the practical:

1. Flee Temptations
Remember, nobody accidentally lusts. As easy and natural as it may be to engage immoral sexual desires in the mind, lust is intentional. So you can and must be intentional about protecting yourself. Identify your areas of weakness and shore them up.

If you struggle with Internet pornography, put a filter on your computer or install accountability software. I use X3Watch, which sends a regular report of Web sites I've visited to partners I've designated (my reports go to my wife, Becky). I've heard good things about the Covenant Eyes program as well.

Unsubscribe from movie channels or from cable/satellite altogether (if necessary). Delete inappropriate apps or Web sites from your "Favorites." Don't go to movies alone. Get rid of those romance novels. Don't put yourself in private, secluded situations with your boyfriend or girlfriend. Find a Christian brother or sister who will agree to ask you tough questions each week about how your battle is going.

 "But each person is tempted when he is drawn away and enticed by his own evil desires" (James 1:14).

As Job did, make a covenant with your eyes (Job 31:1). The call to discipleship is a call to crucify our flesh, which doesn't mean business as usual. We can't go on autopilot and expect to fight the battle of lust on its terms. If you have a friend who's an alcoholic, you'd certainly advise him to get counseling, to address the hurt or brokenness driving him to drug himself that way. But wouldn't you also tell him to get all the alcohol out of his house and avoid bars?

There's nothing legalistic about arranging your life in such a way to avoid temptations. It's not effort grace is opposed to, after all, but *earning*. Sitting at your computer trying not to look at Internet porn will be a losing battle again and again and more and more. So don't just stifle your behaviors, replace them.

What are some practical things you can do to help you flee temptation?

What has kept you from implementing these practices before now?

Of course, doing all of these practical things doesn't get at the root issue of lust, but it will certainly help to level the playing field and show your flesh and the Devil that you mean business about obedience.

In 1 Thessalonians 4:3-5, Paul wrote:

> **"For this is God's will, your sanctification: that you abstain from sexual immorality, so that each of you knows how to control his own body in sanctification and honor, not with lustful desires, like the Gentiles who don't know God."**

The way Paul urged us to participate in our sanctification is by "abstain[ing] from sexual immorality" and knowing how to "control [our] own body." One of the fruits the Holy Spirit plants in our hearts when we receive Christ is self-control. We have this ability. We won't be able to exercise it perfectly, of course, but that's no excuse not to exercise it at all.

By arranging our environment, lifestyle, technological opportunities, time, and more in ways that help us avoid temptation, we're practically cutting out the offending eyes and hands that cause us to sin. As a preacher once told me, when it comes to sin, it's not enough to keep brushing away spider webs; you've got to squash the spider.

....

 "What does God have for those of us who have squandered His grace in the past? . . . More grace." —Ray Ortlund[4]

2. Behold a Better Vision

But the real spider isn't just movies, TV, and the Internet. The real spider is the lustful beast within us. If we're serious about killing lust, we must examine our hearts and address the underlying purpose in our immoral sexual desires. That's the spiritual application of Matthew 5:29-30. When Jesus said to pluck out our eyes and cut off our hands, He was telling us to assassinate our idols. Albert Barnes explained it this way in his commentary:

> "His design was to teach that the dearest objects, if they cause us to sin, are to be abandoned; that by all sacrifices and self-denials we must overcome the evil propensities of our nature, and resist our wanton imaginations."[5]

Whatever our affections and behaviors are oriented around is our object of worship—our "dearest object." If "where your treasure is, there your heart will be also" is true (Matthew 6:21), we must abandon every treasure except Jesus.

What "treasures" in your day-to-day life need to be abandoned?

Read 2 Corinthians 3:15-18. How do we change, according to this passage?

The lie we believe about lust in our hearts is that there's real satisfaction, lasting fulfillment, and ultimate gratification in sex. The other side of this lie is that God isn't all-satisfying and Jesus' grace isn't sufficient.

When we lust, we disbelieve that God is enough and that there's joy to be had in Him.

It's much easier to believe these lies when we're not attempting to behold God's glory. Our vision must change. John Piper offered some very helpful words along these lines:

> "Pure, lovely, wholesome, beautiful, powerful, large-hearted things cannot abide the soul of a sexual fantasy at the same time. "I remember as I struggled with these things in my teenaged years and in my college years—I knew how I could fight most effectively in those days. And I've developed other strategies over the years that have proved very effective. And one way of fighting was simply to get out of the dark places, get out of the lonely rooms, get out of the boxed-in places, get out of the places where it's just small me and my mind and what I can do with it, and get out where I am just surrounded by color and beauty and bigness and loveliness . . .

....

Leading a group? Find extra questions and teaching tools in the leader kit, available for purchase at threadsmedia.com/sevendailysins.

"There's something about *bigness*, there's something about beauty, that helps battle against the puny, small, cruddy use of the mind to fantasize about sexual things.

"And then turn it around: it works this way too. We know from experience that if we give way to sexual fantasies and yield to lusts and dwelling on unwholesome things, our capacities for seeing the sky are cut in half. And then cut in half again. And then cut in half again—until you're just a little worm on the ground as your language and your mind is nothing but smut. It can happen to anybody!"[6]

We must behold a better vision than what's sexually exhilarating and ultimately spiritually damning. Getting outside to look at the sky is one way to do this. Another is by staring at God's glory in the gospel of Jesus Christ. Maurice Roberts wrote that "it is the unhurried meditation on gospel truths and the exposing of our minds to these truths that yields the fruit of sanctified character."[7]

The course is clear: Let us fill our minds with so much good news found in God's Word that our vision is overtaken by what God has done to forgive us in Christ and seat us with Him in the heavenly places.

Read Philippians 2:12-13. How do Paul's words contribute to the topic of battling lust?

LUST AND THE LOVE OF GOD

The gospel tells us we're worse than we dare imagine, but loved more than we dare believe. Believe this; I dare you!

When we begin to fill our minds with the better vision of God found in the gospel of Jesus, we see ourselves as we truly are—sinful and deserving of hell, but deeply loved and eternally secured by the grace and righteousness of Jesus. What's more, we begin to see others in a different light as well.

See, lust results in using people—treating them as commodities for our own sexual gratification. People become objectified, reduced to the sum of their body parts or sexual performance (whether real or imagined).

When we give in to lust, we place ourselves at the center of the universe, and everyone else is in orbit around our desires and satisfaction. This is how the sin of lust is also the sin of pride.

But if, in our consuming vision of the gospel, we get to know ourselves and our sins better and therefore get to taste the love of Jesus more sweetly, we'll start to see people as they are: the precious image bearers of God. And as we grow to love God more and more, we'll begin to love our neighbors more and more—which means looking to sacrifice for and serve them, rather than objectify and use them.

The deeper we know the love of God, the less we'll be given to lust.

To know the love of God deeply, then, begins with being honest about your sexual brokenness, addressing it sincerely and radically, and looking at the gospel with the same intensity and desire as you would a lesser, less-gratifying vision.

The good news is that Jesus lived a blameless life. He was tempted as we are, yet without sin. He died in our place and was raised for our future glorification. And if you'll repent and believe in Him, His perfect obedience is counted as yours. If you'll believe that news, as the Bible says, "in your heart," it will give you real power to conquer lust.

THROUGH THE WEEK

> **Study:** Commit to studying the opposite of lust by reading through 1 Corinthians 13 every day this week. As you read, focus on these questions:

1. What are these verses asking me to do?
2. What are these verses asking me to be?
3. What does it mean to love another person?

> **Pray:** As you talk with God throughout the week, ask Him to bless you with a greater understanding of your responsibility to love the people around you. Also ask Him to help you experience His love more deeply.

> **Connect:** Who do you know who's winning the war against lust? Set up a time to meet with one or more of these people and talk about strategies that could work for you. (It's best to meet with people of the same gender as you.)

NOTES

SESSION THREE

"For I have often told you, and now say again with tears, that many live as enemies of the cross of Christ. Their end is destruction; their god is their stomach; their glory is in their shame. They are focused on earthly things, but our citizenship is in heaven, from which we also eagerly wait for a Savior, the Lord Jesus Christ. He will transform the body of our humble condition into the likeness of His glorious body, by the power that enables Him to subject everything to Himself" (Philippians 3:18-21).

Gluttony is the big fat elephant in the room of the evangelical church. I don't remember ever hearing a sermon or lesson on gluttony when I was growing up, despite the fact it was rampant all around us. I remember plenty of talk on the dangers of sex and alcohol—even rock and roll music—but nary a word on over-indulging in food.

I grew up in a traditional Bible Belt environment, and while the church of my childhood was more "contemporary" than most, we still made no compromise when it came to potlucks, dinners on the ground, ice cream socials, and the like. We were from the South. We were supposed to eat, buddy. On top of that, I come from a border town in South Texas. So if we weren't in the mood for fried chicken, biscuits, and sweet tea, there was plenty of Tex-Mex to be had. The *botana* platter at Garcia's was a gift from Dios Himself. And my dad, summoning the spirit of the half of him that's Hispanic, could cook the daylights out of some fajitas, y'all.

But I digress.

Can you tell I like food? I like it a lot. I've struggled with all seven of the deadly sins off and on throughout the course of my life. But next to lust, gluttony is the sin I've battled (and continue to battle) most.

If you've ever given much thought to combating this sin, you've probably run into the same problem I have: There doesn't seem to be much help out there.

Certainly the sentiments of the world aren't going to do us any favors. We live in the land of all-you-can-eat buffets, Big Gulps, and super-sizing. When portions at restaurants aren't big enough to feed three people, we feel cheated. We've even turned eating into a competitive sport, with one of the umpteen ESPN stations broadcasting battles to see who can eat the most hot dogs!

Taking things one step further, consider this insight from C. S. Lewis in *Mere Christianity*:

> "You can get a large audience together for a strip-tease act—that is, to watch a girl undress on the stage. Now suppose you came to a country where you could fill a theatre by simply bringing a covered plate on to the stage and then slowly lifting the cover so as to let every one see, just before the lights went out, that it contained a mutton chop or a bit of bacon, would you not think that in that country something had gone wrong with the appetite for food?"[1]

Lewis was intentionally being facetious, and he wasn't even writing about gluttony—he was highlighting the dysfunction we don't see in our sexual lust. But if he were alive today, surfing the TV channels with you or flipping through a magazine, I wonder if he'd be astounded to see that strip-teases of food actually exist.

Perhaps he couldn't imagine his illustration would someday reflect reality, but here we are, being tantalized and aroused by the gleaming juices of delicious steaks, the architectural splendor of some well-stacked mega-burger, the whole-life-fulfillment promised by chocolate mousse—all airbrushed and lit up and presented with expertly selected music and pitched by a celebrity or model.

Remember that question: "Would we not think that in this country something had gone wrong with the appetite for food?" The answer is yes, of course. We live in a world where we're encouraged to never stop consuming—be it food or anything else. In our culture's estimation, there's no such thing as "enough."

What recent commercials would count as a "strip-tease" for food?

So, we don't get much help from our culture when it comes to battling gluttony, but we don't get much help from the church, either. This is surprising because gluttony is a major problem for many Christians—especially when we allow the definition of gluttony to expand beyond food (more on that in a minute).

In his book about the Seven Deadly Sins, Billy Graham wrote of gluttony: "It is a sin that most of us commit, but few of us mention. It is one of the prevalent sins among Christians."[2]

WHAT IS GLUTTONY?

At its core, gluttony is about dissatisfaction. Not all dissatisfaction is bad, of course. But given all the good gifts we have in the developed world and the reality that most of us don't have to worry too much about where our next meal will come from, it's profoundly selfish of us to complain that we don't have enough.

In a broad sense, then, gluttony isn't only about food. Just as we can lust for things other than sex, we can over-consume things other than food. In my struggle, gluttony rears its head most evidently when it comes to my diet, but it's also there when I entertain a sense of entitlement about other things.

Look through the infographic "What America Spends on Food and Drink" at *flowingdata.com*.

For example, why am I crushed when I can't sit next to an empty seat on an airplane? It's because I don't want to be satisfied with what everybody else has. Why do I want every vacation to go perfectly, and why do I feel personally hurt when little things go awry? Because I'm not satisfied to be away with my family doing something fun. It must also be complication-free. Why, when thanked and encouraged by people after preaching a sermon, do I wonder why more people didn't do the same? Because I'm a glutton.

So, a broad definition of gluttony would be consuming more of anything than you should. It's a refusal to say "enough."

Whether food or not, nearly everyone struggles with saying "enough" to something in their lives. What is yours?

Why do you think you struggle with satisfaction in this area?

The Bible takes a more narrow approach with gluttony, connecting it primarily with food. (Gluttony is often paired with drunkenness, as well, since eating and drinking go hand in hand.) For example, when the Pharisees chastise Jesus for sharing meals with sinners, they accuse Him of being a "glutton and a drunkard" (Matthew 11:19; Luke 7:34).

But that doesn't mean the biblical solution for gluttony is simply to eat less. Consider what Paul wrote in 1 Corinthians 10:31:

> **"Therefore, whether you eat or drink, or whatever you do, do everything for God's glory."**

Doing things "for God's glory" means making sure that He's recognized as God and praised as God in whatever we do. This means we can't eat or drink or do anything else as if we're the center of the universe, because that glorifies us, not God.

Avoiding gluttony, then, doesn't mean subsisting on bread and water or eating our meals with frowns on our faces. In fact, if we mean to glorify God when we eat, we *ought* to enjoy food, because it demonstrates taking pleasure in something good God has provided. When you give someone a gift, don't you want them to enjoy it?

Essentially, gluttony is making food a drug. When we engage in gluttony, we expect food to provide a pleasure beyond its design. We expect it to help us avoid the problems of life. Or we treat it like an entitlement or as a cure for anxiety.

 "The dilemma posed by consumerism is not the endless manufacturing of desires, but the temptation to settle for desires far below what we were created for."[3] —Skye Jethani

Where did the phrase "comfort food" come from? As it pertains to food that's delectable to eat, that evokes pleasant memories from our past, or satisfies our hunger in unique ways, comfort food is a good thing. But many people remember a time in adolescence when Mom or Dad would prescribe food as the cure for hurt feelings or a bad day.

Again, there's nothing wrong with taking pleasure in good food or treating ourselves now and again. But a steady practice of this kind of diet can create an unhealthy relationship with food. Today, many adults find it hard to cope with hardships or hurts without over-indulging in food, in part because they were trained as children to use food as a way to feel better.

In this way, gluttony is idolatry. By orienting our behavior, thinking, and affections around food, we seek to find in food what can only be found in God.

Read Nehemiah 8:1-12. What are the people commanded to do in verses 9-10?

Why are they told to do this?

According to this passage, what things must take place before we're able to "have a great celebration" with "rich food" and "sweet drink"?

Eating for God's glory essentially means making sure we've put food in its right place. In the passage from Nehemiah above, the people were released to feast on rich food and drink. But this occurred after they understood what the Law said, and they deeply felt the consequences of their sin. Indeed, gospel-fueled enjoyment of good things like food and drink is only possible after gospel-fueled brokenness over our sin.

GLUTTONY DIAGNOSTICS
Take a minute to ask yourself the following diagnostic questions. You don't have to write down your answers or share them with your group—unless your group is designed to be a safe place to confess sin and receive biblical counsel—but be honest with yourself.

1. Look at your bank or credit card statement. Have you spent more money on eating out and buying food than you planned?
2. Do you regularly eat until you're uncomfortable?
3. When you eat out with others, do you find yourself worrying about whether someone else's meal is better or bigger than yours?

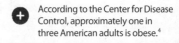
According to the Center for Disease Control, approximately one in three American adults is obese.[4]

4. Is one of your first thoughts in the morning what you plan to eat throughout the day or what restaurant you want to go to?
5. If you use social networking sites, what percentage of your daily updates are related to food?
6. Do you use food as "medicine" when you're feeling bad?
7. Are you overweight?
8. When you finish a meal, do you often feel "gross" physically or emotionally? Do you feel a sense of guilt or shame?
9. Do you hide food at home or in the office? If so, is it because you don't want others to know what you're eating? Is it because you don't want to share?
10. Do you eat mindlessly, losing track sometimes of how much you're eating?

Answering yes to any of these questions could be an indication of trouble spots for you when it comes to food. Answering yes to more than three of these questions is a warning sign that gluttony, in general, may be a problem for you.

Besides raising an alert, another purpose of these diagnostic questions is to help you identify areas of vulnerability and potential idolatry. You can't apply the gospel to a sin you aren't aware of—or one you aren't owning up to. If these questions have helped you reach some honesty with yourself about gluttony, take heart. God wants you to be satisfied.

A HOLLOW JOY

Have you ever had Turkish Delight? C. S. Lewis symbolized the forbidden fruit with this delectable delicacy in his classic book *The Lion, the Witch, and the Wardrobe*. Turkish Delight is what the White Witch used to lull Edmund into betraying his siblings.

> "While he was eating the Queen kept asking him questions. At first Edmund tried to remember that it is rude to speak with one's mouth full, but soon he forgot about this and thought only of trying to shovel down as much Turkish Delight as he could, and the more he ate the more he wanted to eat, and he never asked himself why the Queen should be so inquisitive."[5]

Edmund kept eating until it was all gone. And then the Witch used his hunger for more to keep deceiving him. Edmund was a willing participant because he had given himself over to the god of his belly (Philippians 3:19).

In the end, though, like the forbidden fruit in the garden of Eden, the promise proved empty. Edmund had eaten all the Turkish Delight; the Witch promised him more if he would only keep to her infernal scheme.

....

 Look up the YouTube clip of Francis Chan eating a Snickers bar "to the glory of God."

When he was reunited with his younger sister, he felt differently:

> "'I say,' said Lucy, 'you do look awful, Edmund. Don't you feel well?'
> 'I'm all right,' said Edmund, but this was not true. He was feeling very sick."[6]

Food is good. It's supposed to be. God designed it that way. As I write this very sentence, my wife is in the kitchen preparing her secret recipe pork chops. The tangy scent of the spices and meat sizzling on the stove tickles my nose. My mouth is watering, and my stomach is growling. Praise God for good food and people gifted to cook it well!

The Bible says a lot about food and the enjoyment of food. There are even places where God's people are commanded to enjoy food—like the series of feasts and festivals the children of Israel were commanded to observe each year as part of the Law. Plus, the Bible often equates the abundance of food and drink with God's blessings and the lack thereof with His consternation.

At different points in the biblical narrative, we see food playing important roles in the turning points of people's lives and in God's demonstration of His faithfulness. Think of everything from Esau's trading of his birthright for a bowl of soup (Genesis 25:29-34) to Elijah and the widow making cakes (1 Kings 17:8-16)—from Jesus' feeding the 5,000 (Luke 9:10-17) to His Passover meal with the disciples at the last supper (Luke 22:14-23).

Still, as with all of the things God gives us to enjoy, when we fixate on the gift to the neglect of the Giver, our happiness is fleeting and thin.

Gluttony is one of those sins that offers pleasure and satisfaction for the moment but quickly results in disaster. The immediate effects of gluttony can be physical discomfort and/or emotional irritation. The long-term effects of gluttony can be devastating, with potential consequences like financial trouble, lack of contentment, limited ability to serve God, limited ability to trust God—even a lack of taste for the very foods that once tasted so good!

Think over the following words found in Proverbs 23:20-21:

> **"Don't associate with those who drink too much wine or with those who gorge themselves on meat. For the drunkard and the glutton will become poor, and grogginess will clothe them in rags."**

What sort of images does the word gorge conjure up for you?

How do drunkards and gluttons become poor?

Aside from health issues, what other problems can a gluttonous lifestyle create?

We engage in gluttony because we have a desire, deep down, to find delight and satisfaction. To paraphrase Bruce Marshall's famous words about the young man at the brothel, the young man ordering too much at the Taco Bell drive-thru is unconsciously looking for joy.[7]

There's joy to be found in food, but it's hollow; it doesn't last. In other words, food is made for man, not man for food.

THE GOSPEL FOR GLUTTONS
Remember Jesus' words in Matthew 5:29-30 about plucking out our eyes and cutting off our hands if they cause us to stumble? Well, one of the authors of Proverbs used a similar style in Proverbs 25:16:

> **"If you find honey, eat only what you need; otherwise, you'll get sick from it and vomit."**

First things first: This isn't a recommendation for binging and purging. Rather, we need to combat the impulses (and idols) driving our gluttony. But how do we do that?

1. Know the Function of Food
We gluttons expect more from food than it's designed to give. And we prioritize it wrongly. Take a look at 1 Corinthians 6:12-14:

> **"'Everything is permissible for me,' but not everything is helpful. 'Everything is permissible for me,' but I will not be brought under the control of anything. 'Food for the stomach and the stomach for food,' but God will do away with both of them. The body is not for sexual immorality but for the Lord, and the Lord for the body. God raised up the Lord and will also raise us up by His power."**

When we open ourselves to the dissatisfaction of gluttony over time, we become enslaved to our appetites. This sort of relationship is out of order.

Listen to "Temporary Fills" by Mandisa
from the *Seven Daily Sins* playlist, available
at *threadsmedia.com/sevendailysins*.

Paul said food is for the stomach and the stomach for food, and both will be destroyed—meaning, both are temporal. It makes no sense, then, to elevate food or our hunger pangs to a place of authority over our wills. The context of this passage in 1 Corinthians 6 is a discussion of repenting of sexual immorality, but the principle remains the same: Food has a purpose, and servicing our prideful self-worship isn't it.

Read John 6:1-14 and 35-66. What strikes you about the behavior of the crowd?

What do these incidents say about the sin of gluttony?

We totally miss the function of food when see it as an end rather than a means. We don't have to stop enjoying food to stop enjoying it too much. In fact, as we practice self-control and eating to God's glory, we end up enjoying food more.

2. Know the Foreshadowing of Food
We're used to following our noses and taste buds to food as if it's the prize at the end of a treasure map. But in the Scriptures, mentions of food are arrows pointing away from temporary pleasure and toward real treasure.

For example, the feasts commanded in the Old Testament are commemorations of God's Word and holiness. In Nehemiah 8:9-12, for instance, the re-gathered people of Israel are commanded to celebrate with fatty food and sweet drink because God had consecrated them through His Word. This was just a temporary celebration (as all food is), but it provided a foretaste of the marriage supper of the lamb, when the shadows of the Old Covenant would give way to the Light of the New.

The Passover instituted in Exodus 12 is the precursor to the Lord's Supper instituted by Jesus the night before His crucifixion. The first meal commemorated God sparing the lives (or "passing over") those whose houses were marked with the blood of the lamb—which points to the saving work of Christ's blood. Jesus highlighted this connection in John 6, before the Lord's Supper was introduced, by connecting the miracle of the feeding of the 5,000 to the idea that His hearers must eat His flesh and drink His blood in order to live.

The list could go on and on. Manna in the wilderness, the widow's cakes, the ravens' feeding of Elijah, the water into wine—all of these and more are spotlights shining on God's role as Provider and His Son's role as Provision.

 For more examples of God's role as Provider, read Exodus 16; 1 Kings 17; John 2:1-12; and Revelation 19:6-9.

How is God the Provider of your food?

Here are the words of Paul in Philippians 3:18-19:

> **"For I have often told you, and now say again with tears, that many live as enemies of the cross of Christ. Their end is destruction; their god is their stomach; their glory is in their shame. They are focused on earthly things."**

When we give in to gluttony, we worship our own satisfaction. Our mind isn't set on the heavenly reality but on the earthly shadows of that reality.

We can regain a proper orientation by partaking of the Lord's Supper with our local church. When we consume Christ's body and blood in remembrance of Him, we aren't just confessing that He died for our sins; we're confessing that we need Him inside of us to live, just like we need food and drink to live. When we take the Lord's Supper, we're admitting that without Jesus, we starve to death—no matter how full our bellies get.

Do you feel a need for Jesus in your life? Do you have a "hunger" for Him when you are outside of His presence?

3. Know the Father of Food
The closer we get to God, the less reliance we'll have on His earthly gifts. When it comes right down to it, gluttony is distrust of God's provision, which is distrust of God's character. When we eat too much, it's a reflection that deep down we don't trust God for joy after that meal—that we don't trust Him for *food* after that meal.

In order to rebuild our trust in God, we need to rebuild our relationship with Him—because to know God is to trust Him. So the more we pursue knowledge of the Giver, the less we'll abuse His gifts. This is what David discovered in his darkest, leanest moments:

> **"All eyes look to You, and You give them their food at the proper time. You open Your hand and satisfy the desire of every living thing. The LORD is righteous in all His ways and gracious in all His acts" (Psalm 145:15-17).**

Such knowledge of our heavenly Father eventually led David to say multiple times, "The LORD is my portion." And this portion is generous. And delicious!

 "Don't you know that your body is a sanctuary of the Holy Spirit who is in you, whom you have from God? You are not your own . . ." (1 Corinthians 6:19).

> "Taste and see that the LORD is good. How happy is the man who takes refuge in Him!" (Psalm 34:8).

Real satisfaction and delight—the things we gluttons are looking for in food—can be found, but only in the Creator of food. He gives us His good gifts to be received with thankfulness and to be enjoyed—but to *His* glory, not ours.

Paul provided our final instruction on how to turn away from temporary satisfaction and toward God—how to live (and eat) for His glory:

> "For Christ's love compels us, since we have reached this conclusion: If One died for all, then all died. And He died for all so that those who live should no longer live for themselves, but for the One who died for them and was raised" (2 Corinthians 5:14-15).

When we're being gluttonous, we're compelled by love for ourselves and the hollow joy of food. But when Christ's love compels us, we no longer live for ourselves but for God's glory. How do we orient ourselves out of gluttonous compulsion to the compulsion of Christ's love? By reaching this conclusion: If Christ died for me, I am able to die to myself.

Gluttony isn't just a consumption problem; it's a belief problem. We disbelieve our way into overindulgence, which means we must believe our way out.

THROUGH THE WEEK

> **Study:** Take a long look at Matthew 4:1-11 this week. Keep the following questions in mind as you read:

1. What is the role of food in these verses?
2. What is the role of fasting?

> **Pray:** For many Christians, praying before a meal is a common (and often stale) practice. Continue that practice this week, but pray specifically that God would help you learn how to eat each meal (and every meal) in honor of Him.

> **Research:** How much do you know about world hunger? Commit to spend some time this week learning more. Research recent famines and food shortages, look up organizations dedicated to fighting against hunger, and see if there are any ways you can contribute.

Leading a group? Find extra questions and teaching tools in the leader kit, available at *threadsmedia.com/sevendailysins.*

NOTES

SESSION FOUR

"The one who loves money is never satisfied with money, and whoever loves wealth is never satisfied with income. This too is futile. When good things increase, the ones who consume them multiply; what, then, is the profit to the owner, except to gaze at them with his eyes? The sleep of the worker is sweet, whether he eats little or much, but the abundance of the rich permits him no sleep" (Ecclesiastes 5:10-12).

Almost nothing else makes us stupid like money and what it can buy.

You don't have to be a Wall Street wizard to know that if you keep spending more money than you're bringing in, you'll end up with less than nothing. But that's standard practice for so many of us in Western culture—individuals, families, and even governments. In a society that hands out credit cards like Tic Tacs, accumulating debt is just par for the course.

Advertisers have become more shrewd about tapping into our covetousness. No longer content to promote their products, they've moved to shilling desires for those products—making them feel like necessities for quality of life. Wheaties isn't just selling breakfast cereal, but the satisfaction of having something in common with "champions." Burger King isn't just selling burgers, but the chance to have it our way; they're trying to sell us a slice of power. Allstate and State Farm have apparently moved on from insurance and are now selling peace of mind.

The various ways we're baited by more and more stuff are really just sophisticated strategies driven by greed—from both sellers and buyers. There's nothing wrong with making money, of course, nor with buying things. Until there is.

The Bible says a lot about money. I mean, a lot. Jesus talked about money and possessions so much you'd think His audience was typically full of rich people. It wasn't, of course. He just knew what's at the heart of every one of us, rich or poor, workaholics or lazybones—the love of stuff.

Perhaps no snare is more common to fallen people than greed.

WHAT IS GREED?
Before we get too far into a discussion on how to battle greed, we ought to determine what constitutes greed—and what doesn't. For instance, greed is *not*:

- Working hard to earn money
- Saving money or investing money in wise ways
- Merely wanting certain things (if you can do so without obsessing over them or being upset if you're not able to get them)
- Having wealth

The Bible actually speaks of wealth in both positive and negative ways. We see wealth held up as a blessing from God, and God instructs us to use wisdom and stewardship in order to achieve it. Proverbs 13:11 promises financial ruin to those employing fraudulent business

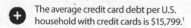 The average credit card debt per U.S. household with credit cards is $15,799.[1]

practices, but growing wealth to the hard working. Proverbs 14:24 speaks of wealth as a "crown" for those who are wise. The Psalms also describe wealth as a blessing from God.

But we're also warned that wealth can be dangerous. If it's not handled wisely and soberly, wealth becomes a curse, not a blessing. Financial blessings are meant to help us enjoy freedom, not become enslaved. That's what Jesus had in mind when He said:

> **"It will be hard for a rich person to enter the kingdom of heaven!"** (Matthew 19:23).

Having said all that, here's how I define greed: Greed is loving money and/or possessions. And I use the word *love* very intentionally.

It's alright to like money and possessions—to appreciate having them. But when we love them, we're investing our affections into things that can't return the favor. We know we've crossed that line from appreciating money and things to loving money and things when our behavior, mood, and sense of self-worth are oriented around money or things.

If you lost all your wealth and possessions tomorrow, you'd be understandably and legitimately sad. But would you despair of life itself? Would it be impossible to imagine going forward without wealth and possessions?

What would happen if you lost all of your possessions today? What steps would you take to move forward tomorrow?

Love involves an orientation of the heart, and we should never orient our hearts around things that don't last. On top of that, love for inanimate objects is pointless.

THE GREED TRAP

Greed didn't start with Wall Street or "vote people off the island" reality shows. It's ancient. We've carried it around in our hearts since Adam. Two of the Ten Commandments speak directly to our greedy impulses: "Do not steal" and "Do not covet." We find this helpful gem in Proverbs 28:22:

> **"A greedy man is in a hurry for wealth; he doesn't know that poverty will come to him."**

It's deceptively easy to get blinded by our desire for possessions. We have dollar signs in our eyes (just like the characters in a cartoon), and we can't see the ruin we're headed for.

 The Bible contains around 800 verses about money and wealth; you can see many of them at *daveramsey.com/church/scriptures*.

Tunnel vision about acquiring money creates such busyness, such a frantic, single-minded pursuit, that it prevents us from properly caring for those around us or even for ourselves. And it certainly keeps us from giving God His due.

In the movie *Limitless*, Eddie Morra is a struggling writer living a hardscrabble existence until he finds a powerful drug that allows him to access 100 percent of his brain. Though it's taken him months to crank out one page of his novel, he finishes the entire thing in one night under the influence of the drug—and his publisher considers it a work of art. So what does Eddie do with this illicit new power? Become the next great American novelist, a mantle he would've gladly been satisfied with before? No. Writing great books isn't thinking "big" enough. He ditches novels and enters the world of finance. Why make a cultural contribution when you can make a currency deduction? He doesn't even wrestle with the decision.

And neither do we. Greed speaks directly to that inner impulse to have "pride in one's lifestyle" (1 John 2:16)—part of what John says is "from the world."

Greed traps us in three significant ways:

1. Greed traps us with its insatiability.
Ecclesiastes 5:10 says,

> **"The one who loves money is never satisfied with money, and whoever loves wealth is never satisfied with income. This too is futile."**

There's nothing wrong with making money (when we make it through honest means), but when making money becomes a primary motivation for life itself, greed takes over. Just like gluttony, greed puts us on a conveyor belt with no stop button and tells us there's no such thing as "enough," only "more."

Many people deceive themselves into thinking they'll stop pursuing wealth once they've gotten "there"—wherever *there* is. But when they arrive at their goal, suddenly *there* has become *here*, and there's another *there* to get to. That's the way of greed. And when we become infected by it, we end up working for money in more ways than one.

Even worse, greed puts us in a position of rebellion against God. Jesus said in Matthew 6:24:

> **"No one can be a slave of two masters, since either he will hate one and love the other, or be devoted to one and despise the other. You cannot be slaves of God and of money."**

Look up the "Saturday Night Live" clip featuring Steve Martin called "Don't Buy Stuff You Cannot Afford."[2] (It's on Hulu.)

When we're greedy, money operates as our boss—which is just a different way of saying that money has become our god. And Jesus is clear: Love of money is hatred toward God.

2. Greed traps us with its related sins.
Greed opens a Pandora's box of sins. Paul warned Timothy this way:

> **"For the love of money is a root of all kinds of evil, and by craving it, some have wandered away from the faith and pierced themselves with many pains" (1 Timothy 6:10).**

This is one of the most famous verses in the Bible, but it has been misquoted and taken out of context by many people over the years. Notice it doesn't say that the love of money is *the* root of all evil, but that it is *a* root of *all kinds* of evil. Certainly it's easy to see how this is true.

My wife and I often watch crime shows like "The First 48" and "48 Hours Mystery," where real investigators piece together the clues to solve a murder or disappearance. I've noticed that nearly all of the cases stem from greed in some form or fashion. From the inner-city kid who wants another's shoes or car to the wealthy heir tired of paying child support, what begins as greed turns into malice, which fuels murder.

When we give ourselves over to greed, we open the door to all kinds of attendant sins. Greed can lead us to justify unethical business practices or outright theft. It can lead us to treat others with jealousy or contempt if they stand in our way or have what we want. It can lead us to disobey the Sabbath command if we refuse to rest from work. It can lead us to worry about non-eternal things, which is the sin of faithlessness.

What other sins are commonly initiated by greed?

What other sins might lead us toward greed?

3. Greed traps us in ruin.
The most vivid contemporary example of this is the incredibly high interest rate on credit cards. It's easy to justify making purchases on credit when we only see the retail price. But once the interest rate kicks in, the more we buy, the more we owe. In a strange way, we're buying debt. We're paying for an item that usually loses most of its value as soon as we take it home—and for the "privilege" of sending more money to the credit card company.

In some situations—necessary medical or vehicle expenses we don't have cash for—credit card debt is a relatively acceptable cost. But in most situations the cost far exceeds the value of what we hold in our hands. For too many of us, debt becomes a black hole that gets harder and harder to climb out of. We can't even relax enough to enjoy what we bought!

Sadly, financial devastation is just one way greed lays a trap for our ruin. It also snares us when we place a high value on money and possessions. The reasoning is simple: When we invest our emotional and spiritual stock in stuff that goes away, we'll be utterly destroyed when the stuff goes away. The stock market may crash; someone may steal everything we have; there could be a fire.

If our heart is where our material treasures lie, our heart will be crushed when those treasures are gone—not *if* those treasures are gone, mind you, but *when*.

Proverbs 11:4 says,

> **"Wealth is not profitable on a day of wrath, but righteousness rescues from death."**

Greed is a trap because it ties us to money and possessions, which tie us to a world that's passing away.

What are some other ways greed might trap us?

GREED DIAGNOSTICS

Because we can be blind to the presence of greed, we need some honest self-reflection to see what the relationship is between our hearts and our stuff. You don't have to write down your answers to these questions or share them with your group—unless your group is designed to be a safe place to confess sin and receive biblical counsel—but be honest with yourself.

1. Are you struggling to climb out of credit card debt because you purchase things you don't really need?
2. When the new version of your favorite electronic gadget comes out, do you buy it quickly or worry if you can't?
3. Does money "burn a hole in your pocket"?
4. Do you spend more money on things you don't need than on giving to church, charitable organizations, or the needy?

 Watch the *Seven Daily Sins* video "Greed," available at *threadsmedia. com/sevendailysins*.

5.   Do you go shopping for things you don't need every week?
6.   Do you cheat on your taxes?
7.   Do you shoplift, steal from the office, or "borrow" friends' things without returning them?
8.   Do you have trouble using vacation days because lost time is lost money?
9.   Does it bother you when neighbors, family, or friends buy things you don't have?
10. Would your neighbors, family, and friends say that money is important to you?

If you answered yes to more than a few of these questions, you have trouble with greed. Study the rest of the session carefully, then, and prayerfully consider how you might become rich toward God.

RICH TOWARD GOD

The kingdom of God operates on a completely different system of currency than any other kingdom in the world. As Jesus unfolds the great blueprint in the Sermon on the Mount, we find Him instructing us to hold stuff loosely. If somebody asks for your shirt, give him your coat, too. Give and lend to whoever asks (Matthew 5:40-42). These aren't ways to become rich—unless the reward we have in mind isn't monetary.

Consider this parable from Jesus found in Luke 12:13-21:

> "Someone from the crowd said to Him, 'Teacher, tell my brother to divide the inheritance with me.'
>
> "'Friend,' He said to him, 'who appointed Me a judge or arbitrator over you?' He then told them, 'Watch out and be on guard against all greed because one's life is not in the abundance of his possessions.'
>
> "Then He told them a parable: 'A rich man's land was very productive. He thought to himself, "What should I do, since I don't have anywhere to store my crops? I will do this," he said. "I'll tear down my barns and build bigger ones, and store all my grain and my goods there. Then I'll say to myself, 'You have many goods stored up for many years. Take it easy; eat, drink, and enjoy yourself.'"
>
> "But God said to him, 'You fool! This very night your life is demanded of you. And the things you have prepared—whose will they be?'
>
> "That's how it is with the one who stores up treasure for himself and is not rich toward God."

In this parable we find a perfect example of a man so caught up in the pursuit of bigger and better—of more and more stuff—that he neglected to invest in things that ultimately matter. All his energy was tied up in improving his property; when he felt that was accomplished, he became lazy and gluttonous.

Does this mean retirement plans are a bad idea? Explain.

For us, the problem isn't with improving our financial state or even enjoying ourselves. The problem is in *only* doing those things, which means we've not prepared for eternity. The man in the parable had stored up treasure for himself, but he wasn't rich toward God. The consequences will be devastating for us if we do the same.

John Piper drove this point home with a real-life parable of his own:

> "Consider a story from the February 1998 edition of *Reader's Digest*, which tells about a couple who 'took early retirement from their jobs in the Northeast five years ago when he was 59 and she was 51. Now they live in Punta Gorda, Florida, where they cruise on their 30-foot trawler, play softball, and collect shells.'

> "At first, when I read it I thought it might be a joke. A spoof on the American Dream. But it wasn't. Tragically, this was the dream: Come to the end of your life—your one and only precious, God-given life—and let the last great work of your life, before you give an account to your Creator, be this: playing softball and collecting shells.

> "Picture them before Christ at the great day of judgment: 'Look, Lord. See my shells.' That is a tragedy."[3]

What happened? This couple is earth-rich but God-poor. When the day of accounting comes—when the kingdom's currency is requested for entrance into paradise—these wealthy, fun-loving, permanent-vacation-taking souls will come up empty-handed.

Jesus warned us:
> **"Don't collect for yourselves treasures on earth, where moth and rust destroy and where thieves break in and steal. But collect for yourselves treasures in heaven, where neither moth nor rust destroys, and where thieves don't break in and steal. For where your treasure is, there your heart will be also"** (Matthew 6:19-21).

 Listen to "Greed" by Shawn McDonald from the *Seven Daily Sins* playlist, available at *threadsmedia.com/sevendailysins*.

Jesus said that whatever is most precious to us will receive our greatest care and praise. And that's why greed is ultimately not about what we do in our jobs or with our bank accounts, but what's in our hearts.

BATTLING GREED WITH REAL RICHES

Look over these various words from Paul:

- "the riches of His kindness, restraint, and patience" (Romans 2:4)
- "the riches of His glory" (Ephesians 3:16)
- "Oh, the depth of the riches both of the wisdom and the knowledge of God!" (Romans 11:33).
- "the riches of His grace" (Ephesians 1:7)
- "the glorious riches of His inheritance" (Ephesians 1:18)
- "the incalculable riches of the Messiah" (Ephesians 3:8)
- "His riches in glory in Christ Jesus" (Philippians 4:19)

What do these references to "riches" have in common? First, none of them refer to financial riches. In Paul's estimation, real treasure is a variety of things that can be summed up in what we receive through the gospel of Jesus Christ—namely, Jesus Christ Himself.

Knowing what the Bible considers to be genuine treasure, then, how can we battle the greed we carry around in our hearts every day? We find some step-by-step help in Ephesians 5:1-14, where Paul revealed four ways we can fight the good fight when it comes to greed.

1. Be Sacrificial

It's true that sacrificing money and possessions can become a legalistic, self-righteous exercise. We all probably know Christians who have decided to "live radically" and are very proud of themselves for doing it. But when sacrificial living is grounded in gratitude for Christ's sacrifice, it becomes a God-honoring, gospel-rich way to better serve others and train ourselves in simplicity and contentment. Look at Ephesians 5:1-2:

> **"Therefore, be imitators of God, as dearly loved children. And walk in love, as the Messiah also loved us and gave Himself for us, a sacrificial and fragrant offering to God."**

God gave His Son for people, not things. And Jesus gave His love to people, not things. Therefore, when we see all the sacrifices our culture pushes us to make for money and possessions, it should wake us up. It should jar us to see how far greed takes us away from being "imitators of God."

 "I think everybody should get rich and famous and do everything they ever dreamed of so they can see that it's not the answer."[4] —Jim Carrey

Are there regular expenses you could sacrifice today? What would happen if you did?

Practically speaking, when we give and sacrifice, we have less time to think about taking and accumulating. More importantly, the act of giving up something we value is like stretching a muscle. By living sacrificially and striving for simplicity and contentedness, we learn how little we really need. And when we do this rooted in "the incalculable riches of the Messiah" (Ephesians 3:8), we find out how rich we already are.

In other words, money loses its luster when we bask in the light of Christ.

2. Be Satisfied
When we're satisfied with Christ, we lose our appetite for sin. And when we find Christ valuable, we lose our appetite for money and stuff. But getting to that point means actively acknowledging what God has done for us in Christ and all the blessings He's already given us. Instead of looking out for more, why not seek contentment with what we already have?

As we continue through Ephesians 5, check out verses 3-5:

> **"But sexual immorality and any impurity or greed should not even be heard of among you, as is proper for saints. Coarse and foolish talking or crude joking are not suitable, but rather giving thanks. For know and recognize this: Every sexually immoral or impure or greedy person, who is an idolater, does not have an inheritance in the kingdom of the Messiah and of God."**

These verses place greed on par with sexual immorality, both of which are idolatry. Notice how the greedy person may be amassing great wealth but has no "inheritance in the kingdom of the Messiah and of God."

What alternative to lust and greed did Paul prescribe as proper for saints? Thanksgiving! He instructed us to be thankful for what we have. And since we have Christ, all we have at this moment is all we'll ever need. Therefore, it should be all we ever really want.

What have you thanked God for in the past week?

How can we "give thanks in everything," as 1 Thessalonians 5:18 says to do?

Satisfaction with Christ produces a radical perspective on money and material goods. The author of the letter to the Hebrews reminded his recipients:

> **"For you sympathized with the prisoners and accepted with joy the confiscation of your possessions, knowing that you yourselves have a better and enduring possession" (Hebrews 10:34).**

How can we be thankful even when someone steals our stuff? By realizing we have a better and enduring possession. Thanksgiving is a powerful antidote to greed because greed tells us we need things, while thanksgiving says our needs are met.

Jesus boiled these thoughts down into a brief but powerful question:

> **"For what does it benefit a man to gain the whole world yet lose his life?" (Mark 8:36).**

The answer is nothing. Money and stuff will never satisfy. But inheritance in the kingdom of Christ (given to you apart from any effort of your own) and your acceptance by the Father (guaranteed by the Spirit and placed in an eternal deposit secured to your heavenly account)—*that* is deeply satisfying. Right?

3. Be Shrewd
If we would truly apply the gospel to our greedy hearts, we must be ruthlessly honest about our desires, relentlessly confessional about our sins, and constantly on guard against the hollow promises of material possessions. If we're given to greed, chances are good we'll be vulnerable to the siren call of advertisers and the status symbols of the culture.

Paul gave us a warning in Ephesians 5:6-7:

> **"Let no one deceive you with empty arguments, for God's wrath is coming on the disobedient because of these things. Therefore, do not become their partners."**

There was a day when the only television my children watched was PBS. This was joyful for me not because of the so-called "educational programming"—what I liked was the lack of commercials. Alas, my kids have outgrown their satisfaction with "WordWorld" and moved on to "Phineas & Ferb" and "SpongeBob SquarePants."

Leading a group? Find extra questions and teaching tools in the leader kit, available for purchase at *threadsmedia.com/sevendailysins*.

The mini-programs between these shows are too much for my kids' developing brains. Many times these advertisements have convinced them they need something they really don't, and many times after that, the item doesn't perform as advertised. Nothing looks the same in our house as it does in the shiny world of TV. What happened? Empty arguments.

What kinds of "empty arguments" are usually most attractive to you?

We've got to be shrewd as serpents in order to combat this stuff. Greed is seductive and intoxicating—be on guard against it. More importantly, be on guard against your own heart. It's deceitful above everything else (Jeremiah 17:9).

4. Be Sanctified

As I mentioned before, beholding the gospel of Jesus in its astonishing glory is what empowers us to kill our idols and love God more deeply. To battle greed, then, it's important that we park ourselves where the only real power is: the good news of Jesus.

As we round out our instruction from Ephesians 5 on this matter, meditate on and savor verses 8-14:

> **"For you were once darkness, but now you are light in the Lord. Walk as children of light—for the fruit of the light results in all goodness, righteousness, and truth—discerning what is pleasing to the Lord. Don't participate in the fruitless works of darkness, but instead expose them. For it is shameful even to mention what is done by them in secret. Everything exposed by the light is made clear, for what makes everything clear is light. Therefore it is said: Get up, sleeper, and rise up from the dead, and the Messiah will shine on you."**

The good news is that sanctification is ultimately God's work. He has shined in us the light of Christ that gives us new life, and therefore we have the ability to repent daily of greed and find satisfaction in Him and joy in the gospel. We can combat greed confidently because "once" we were darkness, but no longer!

As the fruit of the Spirit takes root and blooms in us, it makes us increasingly dissatisfied with the fruitlessness of greed. Repent of greed, then, for Christ offers His kingdom to you.

And He offers it paid in full by Himself.

 The *Random House Dictionary* defines *sanctify* this way: "1) to make holy; set apart as sacred; consecrate. 2) to purify or free from sin."

Think back to the foolish rich man in Jesus' parable. Some people may think: *He should've cared more for others. If he'd given more money away, he'd have the treasure of accomplishing good deeds*. But that sort of savings is a bankruptcy all its own. When we reach the gates of heaven and are asked for the currency of the kingdom to purchase our entry, we'd best not try to hand in our own righteousness.

The Bible says:

> **"All our righteous acts are like a polluted garment"** (Isaiah 64:6).

No, when it's time to enter into everlasting rest, we need only present an empty hand, saying: "I have nothing of my own to offer. But I'm clothed in the righteousness of Christ, which I received through faith and which makes me totally vested in His unsearchable riches. My Savior, in the great grace of God, has purchased my entrance for me."

And, oh—that will be rich.

THROUGH THE WEEK

> **Connect:** Gather some friends and issue a challenge for the week: Whoever can go the longest without spending money is the winner. Ask the following debriefing questions when the challenge is over:

- Did anything surprising happen?
- What was the hardest part about not spending any money?
- What did you like about the experience?

> **Watch:** Pay special attention to any commercials you see this week. How many are advertising products or services that can be legitimately considered a "need"?

> **Pray:** Spend time each day praying about one of the four keys to battling greed found in Ephesians 5: be sacrificial, be satisfied, be shrewd, and be sanctified. Ask the Holy Spirit to keep you accountable and help you grow in these areas.

NOTES

SESSION FIVE SEVEN DAILY SINS

SESSION FIVE

"Then the LORD said to Cain, 'Why are you furious? And why are you downcast? If you do right, won't you be accepted? But if you do not do right, sin is crouching at the door. Its desire is for you, but you must master it.' Cain said to his brother Abel, 'Let's go out to the field.' And while they were in the field, Cain attacked his brother Abel and killed him" (Genesis 4:6-8).

I once heard Matt Kruse, pastor of Seven Mile Road Church outside of Boston, recall a time he was driving out of New York City. At a fork in the road, he took the path he thought best— only to find himself sitting in bumper-to-bumper traffic. From his stationary position he watched in frustration as the traffic in the option he hadn't taken zipped along speedily.

Matt fumed. As his impatience and anger grew, his feelings toward the faceless strangers passing by on the parallel road turned more and more into animosity. Instead of thinking of all the wonderful things he'd experienced on his trip to New York, instead of thinking of the blessing of his family present in the car with him, instead of thinking of all the great things that lay ahead for him—he chose to look to the side, to what others had that he didn't at the moment.

Envy is that "sideways glance," Matt said, and it's a killer.[1]

Several years ago, Gary Thomas wrote about this same sideways glance:

> "Scottie Pippen was born into a small house crammed with a lot of people. He didn't have much as a boy, but his journey into the NBA changed all of that. In 1999, he was riding a contract that promised him at least $14.7 million a year through the year 2002. Together with endorsements, Pippen is virtually certain to walk into another $50 million over the course of the next three years—and that's after already having enough money to own a 74-foot yacht and a $100,000 Mercedes.

> "But it's not enough. A feature in *Sports Illustrated* follows Scottie's thoughts during a pregame warm-up:

>> 'Before every game in Portland's Rose Garden, Pippen only has eyes for one. He'll let his gaze drift over to the courtside seat occupied by Paul Allen, cofounder of Microsoft and owner of both the Trail Blazers and the Seattle Seahawks, a man with a personal net worth of $40 billion. Pippen looks at his employer's geeky exterior and wonders, *How does he do it?* . . .

>> '"He's an amazing guy to look at, man," Pippen says, his voice rising. "What does he have? Forty billion? I want to know: How can I make a billion? I just want one of them! What do I need to do? . . . Tell me how I can make a billion dollars. Tell me how I can become a billionaire."'

"If you asked most guys earning $65,000 a year if they'd be happy bringing in $15 million annually, 99 percent would think that was enough. Yet Pippen doesn't look at his own salary, he looks at Paul Allen's—and suddenly $15 million a year seems paltry."[2]

Envy's sideways glance is a complex snare because it mixes self-pity with covetousness, self-centeredness with desire, and bitterness with the boundlessness of our imagination. Even more, envy is dangerous to our souls because it's inherently disobedient to God's specific command to love our neighbors as ourselves. We're told in 1 Corinthians 13:4 that "Love does not envy." Why? Because godly love is selfless and self-sacrificial; it seeks to invest in others for their good. Envy, on the other hand, is selfish and self-indulgent; it resents others and is at odds with their good.

Envy makes people our rivals rather than our neighbors. Like lust, envy objectifies others, treating them like vending machines to be used—holders of our fulfillment.

How would you define envy?

What would you say catches your sideways glance most?

I mentioned in session one that pride was the original sin recorded in Genesis 1, but it quickly gave root to the remaining six deadly sins. And the first recorded murder in the Bible is rooted in the second sin of the Bible—envy.

Envy isn't mentioned explicitly in Genesis 4's account of Cain's killing of his brother Abel, but it glows radioactively between the lines:

> **"Now Abel became a shepherd of flocks, but Cain worked the ground. In the course of time Cain presented some of the land's produce as an offering to the LORD. And Abel also presented an offering—some of the firstborn of his flock and their fat portions. The LORD had regard for Abel and his offering, but He did not have regard for Cain and his offering. Cain was furious, and he looked despondent.**
>
> **"Then the LORD said to Cain, 'Why are you furious? And why do you look despondent? If you do what is right, won't you be accepted? But if you do not do what is right, sin is crouching at the door. Its desire is for you, but you must rule over it.'**

> "Cain said to his brother Abel, 'Let's go out to the field.' And while they were in the field, Cain attacked his brother Abel and killed him" (Genesis 4:2-8).

God accepted Abel's offering, but not Cain's. Cain had put a great deal of effort into his offering; it was the fruit of his agricultural labors. He felt slighted by God. Abel had God's favor, and Cain did not. So Cain burned against his brother. He wanted what his brother received: the Lord's approval. His envy turned to wrath, and his wrath turned to murder.

This process is echoed in the New Testament by James, who wrote:

> "For where envy and selfish ambition exist, there is disorder and every kind of evil" (James 3:16).

The self-glorification of pride is a doorway to the others-hating nature of envy. And envy is a doorway to theft, lust, adultery, bitterness, malice, and murder. Worse, envy is a shrewd enemy because it passes itself off as being on our side.

WHAT IS ENVY?

Envy is resentful desire for what someone else has or is. This means that envy isn't simply about stuff; it's also about character traits, gifts, blessings, families, positions in life, and more. I can be equally as envious of you because you own a Mercedes as I can because you make friends easily.

The qualifier *resentful* is key to understanding envious desire. Titus 3:3 lumps envy in with malice, hate, and "detesting one another." James 3:14 qualifies envy as "bitter." The implications seem clear: Envy involves a negative feeling toward the person who has or is what we want or want to be. In other words, envy doesn't just want what someone else has or is—it doesn't want that someone else to have or be it *either*.

We learn in Matthew 27:18 that the religious leaders turned Jesus in to be arrested, tortured, and crucified because they envied Him. They weren't just jealous of His following or His power; they didn't just covet His ministry and reputation. They wanted Him dead.

In this sense, as easy as it is to envy, it's also completely irrational. I like what J. R. Miller wrote on this subject: "Envy is a most unworthy passion. It is utterly without reason. It is pure malevolence, revealing the worst spirit. Cain was angry with Abel, because he was good."[3]

In what ways is envy irrational?

....

 The *Random House Dictionary* defines *malevolence* as "wishing evil or harm to another or others; showing ill will; ill-disposed; malicious."

How does envy demonstrate malevolence?

The irrational nature of envy reveals just how ridiculously idolatrous it is. Envy is one fist shaken at God in defiance and the other poised in militant self-assertion. When we're envious, we imagine ourselves as gods, rulers of what ought to be, determiners of whose will should be done on earth—namely, ours.

There are two key ways envy assumes divine prerogatives that belong only to God. First, envy is ultimately about self-honor. "I should have that or be that," we say, reasoning from what we imagine we deserve. We don't see ourselves as falling short of God's glory, but as being denied the glory and honor we deserve. Envy is a way of denying our need to be justified before God and affirming our blasphemous belief that we need no justification— only honor and satisfaction.

Second, envy is about self-sovereignty—about the need for control over what's right and wrong, just and unjust. When we're envious, we're making determinations about what people should or shouldn't have. Cain hated Abel both because Abel's offering was accepted and because his own wasn't. By unleashing the wrath that only belongs to God, Cain asserted his own sovereignty in a perversion of justice.

At the most basic level, then, envy is forgetfulness of God's will and provision. It's fundamentally blasphemous and therefore fundamentally dangerous—especially because we find ourselves slipping into it quite easily.

Why is it dangerous to be forgetful about God?

ENVY DIAGNOSTICS
Envy can look and feel like many different things; it's an excellent chameleon.

Sometimes envy of those who have money masquerades as crusading for those who don't. Or envy of someone's gifts disguises itself as helping the ungifted. There are lots of otherwise good things that can become tainted when done out of envy. Many people get good at passive-aggressive behavior because of the subtle hold envy has on their hearts.

Because envy is sly and self-justifying, it's important that we ask ourselves penetrating questions in order to search out its presence in our hearts. Here are some examples.

 "If we live by the Spirit, we must also follow the Spirit. We must not become conceited, provoking one another, envying one another" (Galatians 5:25-26).

You don't have to write down your answers or share them with your group—unless your group is designed to be a safe place for confession and biblical counsel—but be as honest with yourself as you can.

1. Have you ever been confronted about treating rich, educated, good-looking, popular, or talented people poorly?
2. Whether it's been noticed by others or not, do you find yourself having negative feelings toward a certain person or group of people without a reasonable cause?
3. Do you find yourself despising or otherwise looking down on celebrities on the covers of tabloid magazines?
4. Are you prone to judging people according to their appearances?
5. Do you sometimes feel threatened by people with similar looks, gifts, jobs, or callings as you?
6. Do you often "size up" other people in a room, measuring how they compare with you according to appearance, stature, or position in society?
7. Is it difficult for you to enjoy the successes of others?
8. Do you tend to "stew" on the idea that some people have blessings you don't think they deserve?
9. Look up the word *schadenfreude*. (Don't worry; it's not obscene.) Do you engage in this?
10. Are you nagged by a constant feeling of discontentment?

Answering yes to one or two of these questions doesn't mean you have a problem with envy, but it's certainly cause for closer inspection of your heart. Ask God to help you see if the roots of envy are present there, hidden where you can't see them. If you answered yes to more than three of these questions, there's no doubt about it: Envy has you in its grip. So it's time to get a crushing grip on envy.

ENVY, JEALOUSY, AND THE JEALOUSY OF GOD
When I first began to study the sin of envy, I wondered if there was a real difference between envy and jealousy. Most people use those words synonymously. Both terms are found in the Bible, and there appears to be some overlap between them. But my research revealed a slight difference between envy and jealousy—namely, that envy is always bad while jealousy can sometimes be good.

Envy involves wanting what someone else has or is and not wanting that someone else to have or be it either—it's fueled by resentment. Jealousy is simply wanting what someone else has or is. John Mabray writes: "Coveting is wanting what another person has; envy is wanting the other person not to have it: 'If I can't have it, neither should you!'"[4] (Mabray is using "coveting" as a synonym for jealousy—desiring what someone else possesses.)

....

 Watch the *Seven Daily Sins* video "Envy," available for purchase at *threadsmedia.com/sevendailysins*.

The words translated *jealousy* and *envy* in the Scriptures appear to support this distinction. The word most often translated *envy* in the Old Testament has the sense of "jealousy with a passion greater than wrath" and is most frequently cited as a sin of man. On the other hand, the word most often translated *jealous* in the Old Testament is almost exclusively connected with the character of God. In the New Testament, envy is always condemned, while jealousy is sometimes condemned and sometimes commended, depending on the context.

Envy, then, appears to always have negative connotations. But while there's a sinful jealousy that's very much like envy, there's a *good* kind of jealousy, too.

Have you ever experienced a good kind of jealousy? If so, when?

When we think about the subtle distinction between envy and jealousy, we start to see how the qualifier *resentful* is key to seeing why envy is sinful. There are certainly ways of wanting what someone else has or is that aren't sinful.

For instance, my friend Ray Ortlund has a powerfully joyful presence. His face seems to glow, and that's not just his enduring California beach boy good looks. When you talk to Ray, you come away feeling extremely blessed.

I want to be like that. I want what Ray has—and that's OK. As long as I don't wish Ray harm for having what he has, and as long as I'm ultimately satisfied with Christ, there's nothing wrong with aspiring to the good qualities we see in others. Of course, I can never be Ray, and it would be a sin to want to be the best version of somebody other than myself, because God made me to be *me*.

Similarly, it's not a sin to identify accomplishments or characteristics of others that would be beneficial to have ourselves. And the same can even apply to the things they own. I live in New England, and I have many friends who own generators for their homes in case of power failures. I see how beneficial it would be to own a generator in a climate like ours, and it's not a sin to want a generator like my friends'—so long as I don't resent them for having one while I don't (or want to steal what belongs to them).

In the Scriptures, jealousy takes on an even more passionate positivity. We can all understand the righteous desire a husband feels for his wife; he's jealous for her affection. This can go wrong, of course, but in itself it's a very good, God-honoring passion. Similarly, Paul spoke of the "godly jealousy" (2 Corinthians 11:2) he had for the church at Corinth, because he wanted their affections to be bound up only in Christ and nowhere else.

 Here are a few verses that refer to jealousy in a positive way: Deuteronomy 4:23-24; Joel 2:18-19; Romans 11:13-16.

But the clearest case of good jealousy we see in the Bible belongs to God:

> "You are never to bow down to another god because Yahweh, being jealous by nature, is a jealous God" (Exodus 34:14).

God is zealous for His glory and jealous over His people's hearts. He wants us all to Himself. And the best way to kill the resentful jealousy in our hearts is to realize that God is jealous for *us* in His.

What emotions do you experience when you reflect on the fact that God is jealous about you?

In what way does accepting God's jealousy for you allow you to battle envy?

DON'T ENVY SOMEONE—OWE THEM

Paul mentioned the bad kind of jealousy in Romans 13:13 as part of an epic passage that envisions the kingdom life of kingdom-minded people. Read Romans 13:8-14:

> "Do not owe anyone anything, except to love one another, for the one who loves another has fulfilled the law. The commandments: Do not commit adultery; do not murder; do not steal; do not covet; and whatever other commandment—all are summed up by this: Love your neighbor as yourself. Love does no wrong to a neighbor. Love, therefore, is the fulfillment of the law.
>
> "Besides this, knowing the time, it is already the hour for you to wake up from sleep, for now our salvation is nearer than when we first believed. The night is nearly over, and the daylight is near, so let us discard the deeds of darkness and put on the armor of light. Let us walk with decency, as in the daylight: not in carousing and drunkenness; not in sexual impurity and promiscuity; not in quarreling and jealousy. But put on the Lord Jesus Christ, and make no plans to satisfy the fleshly desires."

Which of the commands in this passage stuck out to you?

 Listen to "Open My Hands" by Sara Groves from the *Seven Daily Sins* playlist, available at *threadsmedia.com/sevendailysins*.

How might it be helpful to think of yourself as "owing" others love?

When we're wrapped up in envy, we think of ourselves as being owed. We may not believe somebody is obligated to give us what they have, of course, but essentially envy is the result of believing we deserve what someone else has or is—and they don't. So envy always puts us in a position of taking.

Paul suggested we reverse our thinking. Instead of envying others, Paul said we ought to think of ourselves as owing them. They're not in our debt; we're in theirs. If we think of ourselves as owing love to others, rather than being owed, we wind up set to a mode of giving rather than taking.

In other words, we can't envy other people if we're too busy seeing ourselves as indebted to them.

Arriving at such a place requires radical humility. That's why Paul commanded us to "put on the Lord Jesus Christ" (Romans 13:14). It sounds like a lofty command at first, but in Philippians 2, we get a glimpse of what putting on Christ really looks like:

> **"Make your own attitude that of Christ Jesus, who, existing in the form of God, did not consider equality with God as something to be used for His own advantage. Instead He emptied Himself by assuming the form of a slave, taking on the likeness of men. And when He had come as a man in His external form, He humbled Himself by becoming obedient to the point of death—even to death on a cross" (Philippians 2:5-8).**

That's a tough example to follow. But in the long run, we'll receive riches through Christ. Surpassing glory. Eternal satisfaction. This is more than a match for whatever temporal things we find ourselves envying in our flesh. When we truly grasp how much we receive in Jesus—in Him we receive all He has—we stop worrying about our lack of anything else.

BATTLING ENVY
So let's put on "the armor of light" (Romans 13:12) and make war on envy. Here's how:

1. Get real perspective.
It's a familiar storyline in the crime statistics: A young man murders someone because he wants his expensive sneakers. The irrationality of envy has taken over. In envy's perverted economy, shoes are worth more than human life. This perspective is clearly out of whack.

Before we congratulate ourselves for being above such heinous crimes, we must get a reality check. The truth is that we all play what Stephen Altrogge calls the "if only" game.

> "Here's how the 'if only' game works. Think about what would make you happy. I mean really, freakishly, 'I can't believe this is happening to me' happy. What do you obsess about, dream about, desperately hope for?

> "Now put the words 'if only' in front of that dream. *If only I could get married, then I would be really happy. If only I could get the job promotion that would get me out of cubicle-land and into the corner office, then I would be satisfied. If only my wife weren't sick so often . . . If only my son would start respecting me . . . If only my budget wasn't so tight, then I'd have peace, joy, contentment, and some sleep at night.*

> "Most people are good at playing the 'if only' game. The only problem is, you can never win."[5]

Envy is the result of upside-down values. The kid who shoots another kid for his shoes won't be satisfied with those shoes, but he will want to continue his sinful ways to accumulate more. And it's the same for us—we won't be satisfied when we get what we wish for. We'll just wish for something else. When we play the "if only" game, we're always stuck with the last place medal called envy. But if we adjust our sideways glance to a different kind of comparison, we suddenly don't feel like such losers.

Ecclesiastes 4:4 says,

> **"I saw that all labor and all skillful work is due to a man's jealousy of his friend. This too is futile and a pursuit of the wind."**

In 2011, Hurricane Irene stormed across the Northeast Coast and caused great damage to Vermont, Connecticut, and portions of New York. I remember having a conversation with a woman whose Brooklyn apartment was flooded with waist-high water—the third such flooding she'd endured in a one-month span. She said that after having to clean up thoroughly and have professionals guard against mold for the third time, she was feeling very sorry for herself. Then she looked up footage of Hurricane Katrina on YouTube. Her perspective changed.

Instead of reflecting on what she didn't have (and what others did), she decided to reflect on what she had that others didn't. Sure, her apartment was flooded, but she didn't lose everything. She was alive and safe. Insurance covered replacements and repairs.

All things considered, she had a lot of reasons to be thankful, not mournful.

This is the kind of sideways glance that would benefit most of us. Whenever we feel anxiety or irritation about the quality of our job, house, car, electronics, or what-have-you, we ought to ponder the plight of the urban poor or those in Third World countries who don't know when they'll get their next meal. When we compare ourselves to people truly struggling to survive, we stifle envy.

What helps you maintain a proper perspective during the ups and downs of life?

Still, this kind of perspective only goes so far. There's yet a more enduring counter to envy.

2. Cultivate thanksgiving.
Envy is the enemy of contentment because it's always focused on what we don't have. But if we train ourselves to be thankful, the muscles we flex through envy will deteriorate. "Thanksgiving is envy's kryptonite," says Matt Kruse. "They cannot exist in the same place."[6]

In order to flex muscles of thanksgiving, we may need to develop some new habits. Write little notes to yourself as reminders of things you can be thankful for, or tie a string around your wrist. Listen to a different kind of music on your morning commute. Begin the habit of giving thanks before every meal, snack, and cup of coffee. Incorporate whatever little practices or reminders you think will help you remember to offer thanks to God for who He is and what He's done.

When we intentionally switch our mode to thankfulness, we suddenly see all that God gives us as sufficient because *He* is sufficient. And if He were to take things away from us—our possessions, our job, our health—we'll be in a better position to praise Him anyway. When Christ alone is our treasure, thankfulness for His "incalculable riches" (Ephesians 3:8) gives envy no purchase in our souls.

It's not for nothing that Proverbs 14:30 tells us,

> **"A tranquil heart is life to the body, but jealousy is rottenness to the bones."**

Finally, consider these words from 1 Peter 2:1-3:

> **"So rid yourselves of all malice, all deceit, hypocrisy, envy, and all slander. Like newborn infants, desire the pure spiritual milk, so that you may grow by it for your salvation, since you have tasted that the Lord is good."**

 Leading a group? Find extra questions and teaching tools in the leader kit, available for purchase at *threadsmedia.com/sevendailysins.*

What practical steps can you take to remind yourself to be more thankful?

What is your plan for ridding yourself of envy?

Warning: If you find the Lord good, your longing for stuff will wane. And when you've tasted and seen that the gospel is satisfying, you'll long for pure spiritual milk.

3. Believe the gospel.
The antidote for the self-honor and self-sovereignty that drives envy is rooted in justification by faith and the supremacy of Christ. Like all other sins, envy is fundamentally a sin of pride, and the only way to kill pride is to confess sin, repent of it, and believe in the forgiveness given to us by God's free grace in Jesus.

Consider Proverbs 23:17:

> **"Don't let your heart envy sinners; instead, always fear the LORD."**

How can the command to "fear the Lord" be an antidote for envy?

Flashing back to Genesis 4, why do you think Abel's sacrifice was accepted and Cain's wasn't? Did God just like Abel better? Did Abel know the right religious words or jump through the right religious hoops? No, Abel's sacrifice was accepted, first, because it was the sort of offering God had commanded. Also, Abel's offering of sacrificed livestock best reflected the stakes of making us right with God.

In Hebrews 11:4, we learn that Abel offered his sacrifice "by faith." He trusted that God makes us righteous not through the fruit of our labors, but through our trust in God's labor on our behalf. This was symbolized in his offering of a sacrificial lamb, which pointed to the future sacrifice of Jesus on the cross.

That's how serious sin is; that's how serious envy is. In order to fix it, something must die.

> **"Without the shedding of blood there is no forgiveness" (Hebrews 9:22).**

God required an offering, and Abel brought real sacrifices—the slain lamb offered to God in humble faith. Cain brought the fruit of his hard work, marred by his pride. We can't and won't satisfy the debt of envy through the fruit of our hard work any more than Cain could. In fact, doing so only makes our hard work unrighteous.

No, if we want to kill envy, it will take death. Thanks be to God, then, that Jesus offered Himself as the acceptable sacrifice. The fruit of His hard work culminated with His substitutionary death—taking our place, covering our shame, killing our sin.

In one of the great, glorious ironies of the gospel, it was envy for what Jesus had that drove us to betray Him and nail Him to the cross. But in His crucifixion, He gladly, willingly, humbly, and freely gave us everything. No one is more generous than Jesus. We need not envy Him or anyone else because His unclenched hand freely gives us all things! So said Paul:

> **"He did not even spare His own Son, but offered Him up for us all; how will He not also with Him grant us everything?"** (Romans 8:32).

So, then, envy is not only spiritual suicide, it's spiritual nonsense! Not one of us can add an ounce of satisfaction through a pound of envy. But in the free gift of eternal life there's eternal fulfillment.

The final and best way to assassinate envy, therefore, is to park ourselves at the foot of the cross early and often. Rather than constantly fooling with envy's sideways glance, we ought to be "keeping our eyes on Jesus, the source and perfecter of our faith" (Hebrews 12:2).

Look at Him and His glory, and you'll find rest.

THROUGH THE WEEK

> **Study:** Take a deeper look at 1 Peter 2:1-5. Throughout this week, reflect on the different ways you have "tasted that the Lord is good."

> **Serve:** Intentionally place yourself in a position of giving this week by serving the members of your church and/or community. (If you don't know where to start, talk to the staff at your church to see what needs you can meet.)

> **Connect:** Identify one or more people who possess character traits you admire. Set up a time to get together with those individuals and express your appreciation.

NOTES

SESSION SIX

"Not that I have already reached the goal or am already fully mature, but I make every effort to take hold of it because I also have been taken hold of by Christ Jesus. Brothers, I do not consider myself to have taken hold of it. But one thing I do: forgetting what is behind and reaching forward to what is ahead, I pursue as my goal the prize promised by God's heavenly call in Christ Jesus" (Philippians 3:12-14).

I'm more familiar with sloth than I ought to be, and it's my own fault.

By that, I mean I wasn't raised to be lazy. My dad wasn't a workaholic by any means, but he did work hard. And he worked jobs—a public school teacher and, later, a retail store manager—that required long hours. He did what so many men of his generation were appropriately taught to do: provide for their families. The slothful tendencies in me, if they have any connection to my upbringing, are pure rebellion, not conditioning.

I don't think we need much training in laziness, really. We condition people to be lazy by not conditioning them at all. Laziness, by definition, is easy. And the temptation to do nothing is hardly a temptation; it's just a default setting in our hearts. We must work to make ourselves work, which reminds me of the common dad-ism: "It's supposed to be hard. That's why they call it work."

This has become harder and harder for men of my generation to accept, perhaps because we've seen the toll that being addicted to work has taken on our forefathers. Facing the prospects of heart attacks, obesity, stress, alcoholism, divorce, absence from our children's lives, dwindling employment prospects, and less and less economic prosperity, we don't see hard work as "worth it" anymore.

And again, it's not like we need all that many excuses to coast. The days of hard work being its own reward are pretty much over. We live in a culture that values efficiency, comfort, convenience, and indulgence. While too many of my father's generation and the generation before him poured too much prideful effort into the idol of the American dream, too many of my own have poured too much prideful effort into the idol of not being bothered.

Is it any wonder, then, that Christianity in America is anemic and impotent?

My first mentor-pastor was Mike Ayers of The Brook Church in Houston, Texas. He once told me that to be a follower of Jesus, you must renounce comfort as the ultimate value of your life. But here in the West, comfort is god.

So while sloth has been a problem since the fall of human beings, it seems like an all-out epidemic today.

Where do you see sloth pop up in today's culture?

 Having a mentor (and/or a mentee) is a great way to combat sloth. You can learn more about that process in the study *Mentor*, by Chuck Lawless, available for purchase at *threadsmedia.com/mentor*.

PETER PAN SYNDROME

Reflecting on the statistical evidence for the younger generation's "taking it slow," Michael Kimmel wrote:

> "The U.S. census shows a steady and dramatic decline in the percentage of young adults, under 30, who have completed these demographic markers [marriage, completion of college education, settling into a career, leaving home]. In 2000, 46 percent of women and 31 percent of men had reached those markers by age 30. In 1960, just forty years earlier, 77 percent of women and 65 percent of men had reached them.

> The passage between adolescence and adulthood has morphed from a transitional moment to a separate life stage. Adolescence starts earlier and earlier, and adulthood starts later and later."[1]

Now, there may be some legitimate concerns and other factors causing this lengthening of what once was transitional. Jobs aren't as easy to come by, the culture has shifted its perspective on women in the workforce, the perception is growing that college is unnecessary for vocational success, and many believe marriages last longer when they're entered into at a more mature age.

But even through simple observation, we can see many negative consequences of this delayed adulthood.

Why do you think people are taking longer to "grow up" than they used to?

How has this delay affected your life?

Some cultural commentators refer to this delay in maturation as "adultolescence," mashing up adulthood and adolescence into some developmental limbo. Chances are you have friends or family stuck there; maybe you're stuck there yourself. Others call this the "odyssey years," or more critically, "Peter Pan syndrome."

Here we are—a bunch of young adults refusing to grow up. We're 27, living in Mom's basement, drinking her soda, and playing games on the Xbox 360 she bought us for Christmas.

Many of us feign looking down at those suffering from Peter Pan syndrome, but the truth is different; in fact, we love them. Our culture equally rewards hard work and slothfulness. We celebrate laziness and find it massively entertaining.

For instance, in my high school years, one of the most popular TV shows featured nothing more than two fools sitting on a couch saying foolish things about foolish music videos. And we sat on the couch like fools and laughed at it. Since then, we've seen programs like the one with friends sitting around a coffee house making sarcastic remarks, the one with boy-men practicing random acts of self-mutilation and painful buffoonery, and the one famously about "nothing." Some of our generation's most popular comedians made their mark portraying themselves as shiftless, dumb, pot-smoking cretins.

Here's what all of this really boils down to: It's harder and harder today to battle sloth not just because sloth is so easy to slip into, but because it's largely seen as fun, amusing, and cute. It's widely considered a justifiable and acceptable way to live one's life.

That's the opinion of our culture. In reality, sloth is destructive, dishonorable, and sinful.

WHAT IS SLOTH?

Before I get too far into this survey of slothfulness, I want to define what sloth is. And I want to start by listing a few things that aren't representative of slothfulness.

Stillness isn't slothful. In a noisy, hurry-sick world, regular silence and stillness is a necessity. Jesus Himself "often withdrew to deserted places and prayed" (Luke 5:16). Times of peaceful, unbusy, prayerful meditation on God's Word aren't laziness. God commands us to take the appropriate time to be still and know He is God.

Sabbath isn't slothful. God commands regular rest from our work. We're supposed to work more than we rest, but resting isn't always sinful (and not resting isn't always honorable). Indeed, it's unwise, irresponsible, and disobedient not to rest.

Recreation isn't slothful. As part of God's command to rest and His freedom in the gospel to enjoy the good gifts He gives us, there's nothing wrong with having fun via hobbies, vacations, games and sports, arts and entertainment, good meals, and just plain being silly. In the appropriate measure, recreation is good for us and reflective of the joyous heart God gives us.

Retirement from a job isn't slothful. Quitting a career to go on a years-long vacation is slothful. But those who retire from a paying job to devote their time to productive, industrious, kingdom-minded pursuits are to be commended.

Ecclesiastes 9:10 reminds us that our time before death is short, relatively speaking:

> **"Whatever your hands find to do, do with all your strength, because there is no work, planning, knowledge, or wisdom in Sheol where you are going."**

This helps us see that sloth isn't just about work *per se*; it's about putting our whole selves into every aspect of life. First Corinthians 10:31 says:

> **"Therefore, whether you eat or drink, or whatever you do, do everything for God's glory."**

The unslothful soul is one that glorifies God in work and play, effort and leisure.

So, what is sloth? Sloth is essentially apathy. This can be a mental or emotional quality in addition to something physical. In this sense, sloth isn't just laziness of body, but laziness of thought or feeling as well. Medieval theologian Thomas Aquinas was on to something when he wrote, "Sloth is a kind of sadness, whereby a man becomes sluggish."[2]

As fun as it can be to be lazy, sloth begins from a downcast disposition or attitude—a sort of sadness we can call apathy or ambivalence. The word *sloth* comes from the Greek word for "carelessness," and that's exactly what sloth is: not caring.

In what ways do you see sloth as being connected to carelessness?

In what ways is carelessness connected to lovelessness?

SLOTH'S EFFECTS
Rather than celebrating and encouraging sloth by finding it amusing, we must take an honest look at sloth's effects. They're complex and damaging.

1. Sloth is destructive.
Ecclesiastes 10:18 offers us this pearl of wisdom:

> **"Because of laziness the roof caves in, and because of negligent hands the house leaks."**

 "Sluggards are worse than cowards. Cowards might shrink back in fear of real dangers. Sluggards invent dangers that are not there, and then justify their inaction."[3] —Peter Leithart

Throughout Scripture, we see the destruction that carelessness brings, from the man's flooded house built on the sand (Matthew 7:26) to the deadly punishment for the unfaithful steward (Luke 12:47).

Sloth isn't simply "not doing something"; it's not doing something that's productive, industrious, or helpful to yourself or others. It's not doing something that we *should* be doing. When we think or act carelessly, we prepare the way for danger.

2. Sloth is irresponsible.

The man in Psalm 1 who slothfully "joins a group of mockers"—and here I think of the people who waste countless hours of their time criticizing others on social media or trash talking the children they play video games against over the Internet—is careless about his own soul. He's slouching his way into ruin (Psalm 1:6). Because sloth is failure to seize our days for God's glory, it culminates in eternal destruction—making sloth not just socially irresponsible, but *spiritually* irresponsible.

The "capable wife" of Proverbs 31:10-31 is a great example for us lazybones. She makes productive use of her time. She's practical, diligent, and industrious. In Ephesians 5:15-16, Paul wrote:

> **"Pay careful attention, then, to how you walk—not as unwise people but as wise—making the most of the time, because the days are evil."**

Sloth is making the least of the time—letting it soak up with possibility and opportunity, then mildew. Again, sloth isn't stillness but irresponsible passivity; it's a willful refusal to take every thought captive to the obedience of Christ.

How would you define the line between relaxation and laziness?

What emotions do you experience when you see another person behaving in a way that is slothful?

3. Sloth is hateful.

My friend Amanda was right when she said that sloth isn't just laziness, but a lack of love. When we're careless, we're loveless. We're not loving God, we're not loving our neighbors, and we're not even loving ourselves.

Sloth is self-indulgence, but it's also suicide. Sloth is a limp fist shaken at God, an unconcerned defiance of His sovereignty and His commands, and a feeling of boredom about His love. This is what the Bible would call hating God.

Karl Barth agrees:

> "The man who does not love God resists and avoids the fact that God is the One He is, and that He is this for him. He turns his back on God, rolling himself into a ball like a hedgehog with prickly spikes. At every point, as we shall see, this is the strange inactive action of the slothful man. It may be that this action often assumes the disguise of a tolerant indifference in relation to God. But in fact it is the action of the hate which wants to be free of God, which would prefer that there is no God, or that God were not the One He is . . . "[3]

The man who can't be bothered about God's commands and expectations isn't fundamentally ambivalent about God; he's fundamentally at odds with God. Jesus was pretty clear about this in Matthew 12:30:

> **"Anyone who is not with Me is against Me, and anyone who does not gather with Me scatters."**

If you're not loving God, you're at odds with Him. When we're slothful, then, we're engaging in hatred of God.

Do you agree that laziness is hatred toward God? Why or why not?

4. Sloth is a form of control.
I happened to catch an episode of a talk show a few years ago, and the so-called self-help guru made a rare insight that was right on the money. A wife complained that her husband couldn't be on time for anything. Forget about being early. He was late—always.

The husband defended himself, of course. "It just happens," he argued. He wasn't trying to be late. Things would just get out of control, he would get scatterbrained, and eventually the time when he'd arrive at appointments became completely out of his hands. The host smartly slapped the label of "shenanigans" on these excuses. Despite the chaos on the surface of the man's behavior, his chronic lateness was about control.

Slothful people may have all kinds of excuses for their laziness and lack of attention (Proverbs 22:13). But in the end, their behavior is all about trying to take control of their time—*and everybody else's*. Their casualness belies the fact that lazy people are, in fact, control freaks.

 "The slacker says, 'There's a lion outside! I'll be killed in the public square!'" (Proverbs 22:13).

Sloth is disrespectful of others. It's a great way of insisting that God and everybody else wait on you, cater to you, and revolve around you.

What are some modern examples of sloth leading to destruction?

Do you agree that sloth is hateful? Why or why not?

SLOTH DIAGNOSTICS

Mark Dever offered some basic characteristics of the sluggard mentioned repeatedly in Proverbs:

- He fails to take advantage of his present opportunities.
- He has an inordinate love for sleep.
- He fails to finish what he starts.[4]

With these identifiers in mind, ask yourself the following questions in a spirit of honesty and seriousness. You don't have to write your answers down or share them with your group—unless your group is designed to be a safe place for confession of sin and receiving biblical counsel—but be forthright with yourself.

1. Do you have a difficult time starting projects?
2. Are you prone to procrastination?
3. Do you have a difficult time finishing projects?
4. When people are soliciting help for something, do you try to keep a low profile so as not to be asked?
5. Do you make a lot of excuses?
6. Would you be embarrassed if your employer knew how much time you spend surfing the Web, chatting with friends, or just generally goofing off while at work?
7. Do you struggle to maintain a regular time of prayer and Bible reading?
8. Is your house constantly cluttered and/or in need of cleaning?
9. Do you have a lot of regrets about opportunities you didn't seize?
10. Do you pretend not to notice obvious messes or areas of attention, expecting someone else to take care of them?

Answering yes to one or two of these questions could be an indication of slothfulness in your life, but answering yes to more than two is a flashing red light. It's time to consider the ways of the ant and be wise (Proverbs 6:6).

 Listen to "I'm Only Sleeping" by The Beatles from the *Seven Daily Sins* playlist, available at *threadsmedia.com/sevendailysins*.

A WORSHIP PROBLEM

In her annotations on Dante's *Purgatorio*, Canto 18, Dorothy Sayers deftly diagnoses the apathetic spirit in the heart of the slothful:

> "The sin which in English is commonly called *Sloth*, and in Latin *accidia* (or more correctly *acedia*), is insidious, and assumes such Protean shapes that it is rather difficult to define. It is not merely idleness of mind and laziness of body: it is that whole poisoning of the will which, beginning with indifference and an attitude of 'I couldn't care less,' extends to the deliberate refusal of joy . . . "[5]

Elsewhere, Sayers wrote that sloth "believes in nothing, enjoys nothing, hates nothing, finds purpose in nothing, lives for nothing . . . "[6] She wouldn't be surprised to find that "whatever" is one of modernity's favorite mantras. Sayers pinpointed the problem: Because sloth is essentially apathy, the problem of laziness is essentially a problem of worship.

What kind of effort does it take for you to engage in worship?

This problem goes beyond singing, of course. A failure to worship is a failure to recognize and submit to God's authority—something Luke captured well with the Pharisees' reaction to Jesus' triumphal entry in Jerusalem:

> **"As He was going along, they were spreading their robes on the road. Now He came near the path down the Mount of Olives, and the whole crowd of the disciples began to praise God joyfully with a loud voice for all the miracles they had seen: 'Blessed is the King who comes in the name of the Lord. Peace in heaven and glory in the highest heaven!'**
>
> **"Some of the Pharisees from the crowd told Him, 'Teacher, rebuke Your disciples.' He answered, 'I tell you, if they were to keep silent, the stones would cry out!'" (Luke 19:36-40).**

Sloth is failure to be astonished by God and what He has done in Christ. When we're amazed by God's grace, our hearts erupt in worship, exulting in His glory in song and service, Sabbath and striving. When we truly "get" how sinful we are in the light of how forgiven we are by God in Jesus, the natural response is passion. The result is God-glorifying, Christ-centered, Spirit-filled worship.

But when we're slothful we say, "Eh, God, You're not such a big deal."

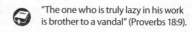 "The one who is truly lazy in his work is brother to a vandal" (Proverbs 18:9).

I like how author Staci Eastin approached this idea:

> "The habit of procrastination indicates a worship problem: an unwillingness to do the work that God has appointed for us, or an inability to discern what He has given us and what He has not. The procrastinator loves to hoard her time for herself rather than work diligently in it on the errands and tasks God gives her. She would rather blame the chaos outside of her than the chaos in her heart."[7]

Eastin helpfully highlighted how excuses factor into sloth's "whatever" culture, demonstrating how laziness—for all its do-nothing-ness—is really a huge self-justification project.

When was the last time you let a responsibility slip because of procrastination? What were the consequences of that action (or inaction)?

When was the last time you felt amazed by God or something He did? What was your reaction?

What gods are we worshiping when we're lazy?

Are you seeing yourself in any of this? Have you identified your sloth problem as a worship problem? If so, draw near to God with confidence through the free grace announced in His gospel.

BATTLING SLOTH
This will be difficult work. Taking up one's cross always is. But there's power beyond yourself to help you in your war on sloth.

Remember that grace isn't opposed to effort, but to *earning*. The sin of sloth may be besetting, but I know Whom you have believed in, and I am convinced that He is able to guard what you've committed to Him. If you've believed in Jesus for salvation, His power is present within you.

So steel your mind. You can't coast into His likeness.

 One way to make an effort in the battle against sloth is to engage in spiritual disciplines, which are the subject of *Abide*—another study written by Jared Wilson. Learn more at *threadsmedia.com*.

D. A. Carson wrote:

> "People do not drift toward holiness. Apart from grace-driven effort, people do not gravitate toward godliness, prayer, obedience to Scripture, faith, and delight in the Lord. We drift toward compromise and call it tolerance; we drift toward disobedience and call it freedom; we drift toward superstition and call it faith. We cherish the indiscipline of lost self-control and call it relaxation; we slouch toward prayerlessness and delude ourselves into thinking we have escaped legalism; we slide toward godlessness and convince ourselves we have been liberated."[8]

Throw out the excuses. Yes, the Spirit is sanctifying you, but He doesn't do it through osmosis. The reality is that you'll not grow in the Christian life through stasis. You must *move*.

But move where? Move how? What is "grace-driven effort" and how is it different from some other kind of religious or spiritual effort?

Grace-driven effort erupts from beholding the gospel (see 2 Corinthians 3:18). Here's one of my favorite passages from Paul. He was talking about doing hard work, but notice how he framed this spiritual effort:

> "Not that I have already reached the goal or am already fully mature, but I make every effort to take hold of it because I also have been taken hold of by Christ Jesus. Brothers, I do not consider myself to have taken hold of it. But one thing I do: Forgetting what is behind and reaching forward to what is ahead, I pursue as my goal the prize promised by God's heavenly call in Christ Jesus. Therefore, all who are mature should think this way. And if you think differently about anything, God will reveal this to you also. In any case, we should live up to whatever truth we have attained" (Philippians 3:12-16).

Write down all the "effort words" Paul used to describe his work.

What does it mean to "live up to whatever truth we have attained"?

What effects will a slothful lifestyle have on a follower of Jesus?

 Leading a group? Find extra questions and teaching tools in the leader kit, available for purchase at *threadsmedia.com/sevendailysins*.

Paul bookended this instruction with something very interesting and crucial to our efforts in fighting sloth. He first said he made efforts because Jesus had taken hold of him. At the end, he said he was trying to live up to the truth that he'd "already attained." Couched in these two past-tense accomplishments, his present-tense effort is revealed as grace-driven.

He didn't "get his act together" in order to keep up appearances, to demonstrate his own powers, to prove something to himself, to climb the corporate ladder, to feel better about himself, to be able to write a self-help book, or because he wanted to live his "best life now." He strove diligently, passionately, and worshipfully because he had the confidence and humility of knowing God had forgiven his hell-worthy slothfulness and had justified him by the blood of Christ.

Think on this: By faith alone, through no effort of our own, God justifies us. *Justifies us!* That's staggering. Put down the remote control and stagger.

Here are your two steps for battling sloth:
1. *See sloth for the sin that it is.*
Hopefully this session has helped you to see that sloth is destructive, irresponsible, hateful, and prideful. If you're deeply grieved about this, you're in the right position to repent of it.

2. *Believe in Jesus Christ for the forgiveness of your sin, full pardon from its debt, the receipt of His righteousness as your own, and the promise of eternal life.*
I've written elsewhere: "Generally speaking, people aren't lazy because they think they're forgiven for trespassing the law; they're lazy because they think the law doesn't apply to them."[9]

But if we know deep down in our bones that the law applies to us, and therefore condemns us, knowing in our hearts that we've been forgiven doesn't strike us as license to be lazy but as cause to dance!

So many of us try to cure our laziness (or that of others) by firing the six-shooter of God's orders at our feet and yelling, "Dance!" But the best means of fueling joyful movement is simply playing the music of the gospel.

When we believe in Jesus with saving faith, the indwelling Spirit is suddenly there, ready and eager to produce fruit through our labors.

Paul wrote:
> **"I labor for this, striving with His strength that works powerfully in me"**
> **(Colossians 1:29).**

If you're flagging, dragging, or slacking, keep Jesus Christ in the forefront of your mind—the glorious, risen, conquering, merciful, providential Savior who loves you and has given Himself for you.

In sloth, we live as if we're God. In the Spirit, we live as if He is.

I'll end with this final reflection from the *Heidelberg Catechism*:

> "Question: What is your only comfort in life and in death?
>
> "Answer: That I am not my own but belong body and soul, in life and in death to my faithful Savior Jesus Christ.
>
> "He has fully paid for all my sins with His precious blood, and has set me free from the tyranny of the Devil. He also watches over me in such a way that not a hair can fall from my head without the will of my Father in heaven; in fact, all things must work together for my salvation.
>
> "Because I belong to Him, Christ, by His Holy Spirit, assures me of eternal life and makes me wholeheartedly willing and ready from now on to live for Him."[10]

THROUGH THE WEEK

> **Study:** Like gluttony, the sin of sloth is often overlooked by Christians today. As you go about your regular Bible study this week, keep an eye out for commands or principles that would apply to slothful attitudes and behavior. (If you would like a sloth-specific jumpstart, consider reading through Proverbs or 2 Thessalonians 3.)

> **Watch:** Take a few minutes to search online for video clips of three-toed sloths. As you watch, consider the connections between sloths (the animals) and slothfulness in human beings. How are they similar and/or different?

> **Read:** This week, commit to reading a book about the spiritual disciplines. Some good examples include:

- *Abide*, by Jared C. Wilson
- *Celebration of Discipline*, by Richard J. Foster
- *Spiritual Disciplines Handbook*, by Adele Ahlberg Calhoun

 Written in 1563, the Heidelberg Catechism was originally intended to be a tool for teaching young people about the Christian faith.

NOTES

SESSION SEVEN

"When they came to Nacon's threshing floor, Uzzah reached out to the ark of God and took hold of it because the oxen had stumbled. Then the LORD's anger burned against Uzzah, and God struck him dead on the spot for his irreverence, and he died there next to the ark of God" (2 Samuel 6:6-7).

To say that the Old Testament was written in blood is barely metaphorical. From the animal skins God used to cover Adam and Eve in Genesis 3 to the promised destruction of evildoers in Malachi 4, the holiness of God was as vivid as crimson. In between, the people of the one true God were sustained and sanctified by the shedding of blood.

Here's a particularly illustrative passage when it comes to God's wrath:

> "Then He said to me: 'Son of man, this is what the Lord GOD says: These are the statutes for the altar on the day it is constructed, so that burnt offerings may be sacrificed on it and blood may be sprinkled on it: You are to give a bull from the herd as a sin offering to the Levitical priests who are from the offspring of Zadok, who approach Me in order to serve Me.' This is the declaration of the Lord GOD. 'You must take some of its blood and apply it to the four horns of the altar, the four corners of the ledge, and all around the rim. In this way you will purify the altar and make atonement for it'" (Ezekiel 43:18-20).

Blood on the four horns. Blood on the four corners. Blood around the rim. Basically, blood *everywhere*. The way to make sure the altar was pure was to meticulously paint it with blood. The establishment of the sacrificial system in the nation of Israel's worship institutionalized ritual death as the means of life.

God's rationale for this arrangement is distilled in Leviticus 17:11:

> "For the life of a creature is in the blood, and I have appointed it to you to make atonement on the altar for your lives, since it is the lifeblood that makes atonement."

The author of Hebrews alluded to this passage, writing:

> "According to the law almost everything is purified with blood, and without the shedding of blood there is no forgiveness" (Hebrews 9:22).

Really, the message couldn't be more clear:

> "For the wages of sin is death" (Romans 6:23).

 "The canon of Scripture shows us tracks of blood from the very edge of Eden outwards."[1] —Russell Moore

This conveyor belt of killing reminds us not just that we do unholy things, but that we're unholy people. Sin is deadly and daily. We carry it around in our depraved little hearts.

What emotions did you experience while reading the previous passages?

How do these passages reflect God's wrath?

What we learn from the sacrificial system and all the mentions of God's anger and wrath in the Bible is that God, who is Love, means business. He's a merciful God, but He's also a righteous and just God. He won't let anything compromise or contend with His holiness—otherwise He wouldn't be holy.

God's holiness isn't confined to Himself. We can see glimpses of it all across the universe, and it was even placed in our hearts (Ecclesiastes 3:11). We were originally made in God's image, and we still carry an echo of God's holiness—an innate sense of what's right and wrong, just and unjust.

Because of the fall of man in Genesis, however, that echo of God's holiness has been distorted by sin. Instead of using God's holiness as the standard for what is right and wrong, just and unjust, we often make a standard out of our own opinions. We set ourselves up as judges and deliver our own verdicts—meaning, human wrath is a result of self-exaltation.

WHAT IS WRATH?

In some writings on the Seven Deadly Sins, the sin of wrath is categorized as "anger." The intended meaning is the same, but I find this connection problematic. While anger is strongly cautioned against throughout the Bible (see Proverbs 15:18; Ecclesiastes 7:9; Ephesians 4:31; Colossians 3:8; and James 1:19), anger by itself isn't always a sin. It's possible to be justifiably angry—something often referred to as "righteous indignation."

Read Matthew 21:12-13. How did Jesus' actions reflect justifiable anger?

In fact, wouldn't it be a problem if Christians never got angry about things like social injustice, violence, sexual abuse, racism, and heresy? The Bible warns us about anger that comes from personal offenses, not anger at the victimization and marginalization of others.

- -

 To learn more about the doctrine of atonement, check out *The Cross of Christ*, by John Stott, and *The Glory of the Atonement*, edited by Charles E. Hill and Frank A. James III.

This distinction is reflected in Ephesians 4:26, where Paul wrote: "Be angry and do not sin. Don't let the sun go down on your anger." The issue isn't with anger *per se*—because, again, some anger is justifiable—but with anger that's *uncontrolled*.

Here's how this concept is expressed in Proverbs 29:11:

> **"A fool gives full vent to his anger, but a wise man holds it in check."**

With this in mind, we could say that wrath is self-centered anger. This definition even works for God's wrath, because God is self-centered—only, for Him, this isn't wrong. God ought to be God-centered! Human wrath, on the other hand, reflects an anger that lacks self-control. The sin of wrath is more concerned with our own satisfaction than with God's glory—which is bad because "man's anger does not accomplish God's righteousness" (James 1:20).

Also, wrath is connected with vengeance. So when it comes from God, wrath is holy and righteous. When it comes from us, wrath is sinful and self-righteous.

Read Deuteronomy 19:15-21.

This passage provides the biblical basis for "eye for an eye, tooth for a tooth." What qualifications and restrictions must be in place before such justice can be meted out?

Do these commands still apply for Christians today? Why or why not?

WHOSE WRATH?

It happened on May 1, 2011—the moment millions of people had been waiting and hoping for over the course of a decade. On that Sunday morning inside a walled compound in Pakistan, United States Navy Seals shot and killed Osama bin Laden.

President Obama announced in his speech on this turn of events that justice had been served. Many Americans breathed a sigh of relief. Many others weren't just relieved, but jubilant. I watched the varying reactions to the news of bin Laden's death in the media, both national and social, throughout the night. Some simply expressed a reserved satisfaction. Others celebrated. Some mocked, some boasted, some reveled. Outside the White House gates a raucous crowd partied like it was the last New Year's Eve ever.

I'll admit that my reaction to that event was mixed. Obviously I was pleased that justice had finally been served. But I was at times uncomfortable with some of the more extreme reactions to the news. I read some tweets that troubled me, for example—wishes that bin Laden would "rot in hell" or receive some kind of personal treatment from Satan.

Looking back, I was experiencing a palpable tension between a good kind of satisfaction in the death of a man who had orchestrated the deaths of thousands with promises to kill more, and a distressing kind of satisfaction in rejoicing over any man being killed.

That kind of tension is also reflected in God's Word. Sure, there are a few passages in the Bible like 2 Chronicles 20:24 and 27:

> "When Judah came to a place overlooking the wilderness, they looked for the large army, but there were only corpses lying on the ground; nobody had escaped . . . Then all the men of Judah and Jerusalem turned back with Jehoshaphat their leader, returning joyfully to Jerusalem, for the LORD enabled them to rejoice over their enemies."

But for each of those, there's another like Ezekiel 33:11:

> "'Tell them: As I live'—the declaration of the Lord GOD —'I take no pleasure in the death of the wicked, but rather that the wicked person should turn from his way and live. Repent, repent of your evil ways!'"

We should rejoice that God is righteous and just. We shouldn't celebrate as if He's not or won't be righteous and just *with us*. Meaning, we mess up when we celebrate or exercise God's wrath in such a way that indicates we don't deserve it, too.

The Scriptures do give us a human outlet for exercising God's wrath—we call it our government. In Romans 13, Paul affirmed that government authorities are from God, instituted by God, and that they "carry the sword" for good reason:

> "Everyone must submit to the governing authorities, for there is no authority except from God, and those that exist are instituted by God. So then, the one who resists the authority is opposing God's command, and those who oppose it will bring judgment on themselves. For rulers are not a terror to good conduct, but to bad. Do you want to be unafraid of the authority? Do good and you will have its approval. For government is God's servant to you for good. But if you do wrong, be afraid, because it does not carry the sword for no reason. For government is God's servant, an avenger

that brings wrath on the one who does wrong. Therefore, you must submit, not only because of wrath, but also because of your conscience" (vv. 1-5).

Human governments reflect the justice of God when appropriate punishments are meted out to those guilty of crimes, and even in the case of a just war. We ought to place an emphasis on "guilty" and "just," however, because Deuteronomy 19:15-21 reminds us of the heavy burden of stewarding justice—we must exercise it fairly, honestly, and uprightly.

How do you react to those verses from Romans 13?

In what ways should Christians "submit" to their governments?

What situations would call for Christians to resist government instead of submit?

Still, we're fallen people. And while God allows our governments and political entities to steward justice—and while He directs our church bodies to exercise discipline—He nevertheless forbids vengeance from finding any place in personal relationships. Here are the words of Jesus:

> "You have heard that it was said, An eye for an eye and a tooth for a tooth. But I tell you, don't resist an evildoer. On the contrary, if anyone slaps you on your right cheek, turn the other to Him also. As for the one who wants to sue you and take away your shirt, let Him have your coat as well. And if anyone forces you to go one mile, go with Him two. Give to the one who asks you, and don't turn away from the one who wants to borrow from you. You have heard that it was said, Love your neighbor and hate your enemy. But I tell you, love your enemies and pray for those who persecute you . . . " (Matthew 5:38-44).

Jesus knows that we carry sin in our hearts. So He commands us to give up our sense of personal justice and take up the justice of the cross, upon which mercy and wrath collide—multiplying the former and satisfying the latter.

It's because of Jesus and His cross that Paul wrote the following in Colossians 3:8:

 Watch the *Seven Daily Sins* video "Wrath," available for purchase at *threadsmedia.com/sevendailysins*.

> "But now you must also put away all the following: anger, wrath, malice, slander, and filthy language from your mouth."

Wrath belongs to God, not to us. For this reason, we must keep a close eye on our anger and dwell in the truth of God's Word daily to provide fertile ground in our hearts for the Spirit to produce the fruit of gentleness, peace, and self-control in us.

When we become eager to enact God's wrath through personal vengeance, it's often because we distrust God's ability to deal with injustice Himself. Or we distrust Him to do it in a way that satisfies us. When we lash out, fight back, take up zealous causes, angrily pontificate, feud on Facebook, tsk-tsk on Twitter, and berate on blogs, aren't we, in essence, saying God needs us to set people straight? All too often what we're really protecting isn't God's honor, but our reputation or influence.

Jesus' approach to personal wrongs would have us conquer the injustice by embracing its satisfaction at the cross. So instead of attacking the guy who takes our shirt, we offer him our coat, too. I'll admit that Paul's questions in 1 Corinthians 6:7 sting a bit:

> "Why not rather put up with injustice? Why not rather be cheated?"

If the cross is true, if God is sovereign—why not?

> "Friends, do not avenge yourselves; instead, leave room for His wrath. For it is written: Vengeance belongs to Me; I will repay, says the Lord" (Romans 12:19).

The reality is that whatever wrath remains to dispense after the satisfaction of the cross will be dispensed by Jesus Himself upon His return. The Book of Revelation doesn't portray a passive, excuse-tolerating King who gives everybody a hall pass whether they love Him or not. Instead, He arrives on a white horse with a sword, vanquishing His enemies. But *He* does this, not us. So if we truly trust that vengeance is His, that He will repay, we have all the power in the Spirit to let it go.

And honestly, that's what some Christians need to do right now: Let. It. Go. Because God won't leave any loose ends.

Do you find it hard to overlook things when you've been wronged? If so, why?

What are the benefits of simply suffering wrong, as Paul asked in 1 Corinthians 6:7?

What are the challenges of letting things go when we're wronged?

WRATH DIAGNOSTICS

Once upon a time, I worked for a couple of men who made my life miserable. They were verbally and spiritually abusive. To make matters worse, they were ministers. I had no recourse for the injustice I felt. Anybody I talked to about the situation seemed to make excuses for them. And I couldn't even get meetings with them to explain my hurt and ask for explanations.

My time with these men only lasted a couple of years. But the hurt this experience caused lasted nearly a decade. My hurt was genuine, the injustice real, but my anger went unchecked, and bitterness festered.

Finally, I woke up one day and realized the only person still worrying about this situation, long since over, was me. The only person suffering from my unforgiveness was me; it certainly wasn't affecting them, and it certainly wasn't bringing justice. In a weird way, by stewing on this injustice for so long, I was giving these fellows more power over me— continuing my ongoing victimization long after they'd dropped out of having any real influence over me.

So I gave it over to God.

On that day, I decided I wasn't going to give those guys power over my heart any longer. I decided that since God had forgiven me at the cross of Christ, it was within my ability to forgive them. And I did. But this process required a gut check. I had to be honest about my desire for vengeance, which was really a desire to be personally vindicated and satisfied.

You might need that kind of gut check, too. Ask yourself the following questions. You don't have to write down your answers or share them with your group—unless your group is designed to be a safe place to confess sin and receive biblical counsel—but be brutally honest with yourself.

1. Do you have difficulty letting go of personal hurts?
2. Are you known for being argumentative and/or defensive?
3. Do people sometimes tell you that you have thin skin? A short temper?
4. When a non-Christian does something offensive, is your first response anger about their sin rather than pity about their ignorance?
5. Do you have to get the last word?

 Listen to "God's Gonna Cut You Down" by
Johnny Cash from the *Seven Daily Sins* playlist,
available at *threadsmedia.com/sevendailysins*.

6. Are there people you haven't talked to in awhile simply because you're angry with them?

7. In arguments with friends, family, or spouse, can you focus on the issue(s) at hand and be reasonable, or do your emotions lead you to say things designed to inflict hurt and "win"?

8. Does the very idea of forgiving somebody who's hurt you make you angry?

9. When you play games or sports, does your "competitive side" take over and compromise your ability—or others' ability—to have fun?

10. If you're in a position of authority over others—employees, athletic team, students, children (yours or others')—do you find it difficult to correct/discipline without venting anger?

If you answered yes to more than a couple of these questions, you likely have a problem with wrath.

WHERE DOES WRATH COME FROM?

When we experience wrath, it often seems to come out of nowhere—almost like an automatic reaction to a person or event. But I think Dallas Willard was right when he said:

> "The explosion of anger never simply comes from the incident. Most people carry a supply of anger around with them."[2]

Here are some of the common reservoirs that can supply us with wrath.

1. Wrath starts with hurt.
The reality is that hurt people hurt people. If you struggle with wrath, it's likely over a real offense you've suffered. It could be the need for payback you feel is aimed at the person who hurt you, but many times our sense of hurt gets spewed out in wrath toward all kinds of people who don't deserve it.

Sometimes the hurt is a big hurt—we were abused, we were unjustly accused, we were bullied. Sometimes the hurt isn't necessarily caused by a person, but it started from a pain we suffered—we lost a loved one, we lost our livelihood, we lost our home in a disaster, we were diagnosed with a disease.

In any event, feelings of unchecked anger nearly always stem from a deep-rooted sense of pain or injustice. Think about it: Someone cuts us off on the highway, and we angrily honk, yell, or make specific hand gestures. Why? It's not just because of the offense of being cut off; it's because of what that offense represents—a series of offenses or one big offense we've not yet learned how to overlook and give over to God.

Anger problems are often pain problems. We haven't learned how to deal with pain, so we lash out and hurt others or become filled with vengeance, thinking this will bring satisfaction. It never consoles the hurt, of course. In fact, it often creates a new cycle of wrath in somebody else.

2. Wrath appeals to entitlement.

Pride is the foundation of every sin, and wrath is no exception. When we lash out or seek payback because of an offense, we're demonstrating our belief that *we are owed*.

And sometimes we are! There are legitimate grievances that deserve addressing. When someone has made us a victim of their own sin, they do owe us a repentant apology. But we should be cautious, because this sense of entitlement can also cause us harm.

It's like the heat gauge on your car's dashboard panel. There are normal levels that represent what we deserve all the time—human dignity, respect of body and property by others, and so on. When someone violates those normal expectations, the needle rises. Suddenly we're in the yellow range. We're seriously owed an apology or restitution of some kind, but we're also in danger of becoming *too* interested in restitution. Like anger, if our sense of entitlement goes unchecked by God's sovereignty and personal self-control (even when it's legitimately aroused), that needle can fly into the red zone of wrath.

The solution is to consider our own sinfulness in the light of God's holiness, which puts any entitlement we might feel on pretty shaky ground.

3. Wrath results from self-idolatry.

When we experience wrath, that needle is in the red. We're hurt, we feel entitled, and, therefore, we must be appeased. Suddenly we're unable to let anything go; satisfaction must be made. Forgiveness? What's that? I'll forgive when they repent! I'll forgive when I know they're sorry, and I'll make them sorry if it's the last thing I do!

Wrath is the product of self-glorification and self-exaltation. Like some all-encompassing god whose needs must be met, wrath takes hurt and entitlement and uses them as justification to usurp the place of God as judge.

This is a big problem for two reasons:

1. We are not God.
2. God has withheld His wrath from us.

Read Matthew 18:23-35.

 "You may be moved, I know full well, and think you have just reason to be angry, and to avenge yourself. But be careful not to do what anger dictates…. For if we are led by anger, it will not let us do any thing right."[3] —Martin Luther

According to this parable, how should the kingdom of heaven affect the economy of personal debts?

Does this point to a change in any of the relationships in your life? If so, what?

Wrath is a willful forgetfulness—a decision to deny others what we ourselves have received. Through Christ, God has let us off the hook. But we're not gonna let others off so easy!

This is dangerous. Because according to Matthew 18:23-35, when we put ourselves in the place of our wrathful God, meting out vengeance however we see fit, we indulge the sin of prideful self-worship. And that puts us squarely in the crosshairs of God's wrath.

BATTLING WRATH
Now you have the diagnosis for wrath. But what's the prescription?

1. Keep a close watch on yourself.
If you know the warning signs, you can stay alert for them. Knowing yourself in this way is the first step toward battling any sin, wrath included. Name your sin, confess your sin, and pray against your sin.

Ask God to show you the roots of your wrath. Ask others to help you see where your weaknesses are when it comes to wrath. Do certain things provoke you more than others? Do certain situations tempt you to become wrathful more than others? Identify those and take appropriate steps to maintain your awareness and put up your guard.

Paul identified the breeding grounds for and the symptoms of wrath in Ephesians 4:31:

> **"All bitterness, anger and wrath, shouting and slander must be removed from you, along with all malice."**

Are you bitter? Explore why and meditate on the forgiveness of God.

Are you angry? Identify why and meditate on the peace of God.

Are you given to insults and sarcastically picking on others? Figure out why, then repent.

 The Book of James offers great advice for dealing with the symptoms and consequences of uncontrolled anger (especially chapters 1 and 4).

Do you feed your wrath with angry music, violent movies, negative news stories, cynical friends, and so on? Get to the root of your wrath problem and be proactive about curbing the negative influences harming you in this area.

We've been forgiven a huge debt. And when we don't forgive—when we engage in wrath—it's like slapping God in the face. It's like looking at the cross of Christ and saying, "Eh, no big deal."

2. Take the right orders.
Many times our wrathful thoughts, words, and actions are the result of pursuing justice. We consider ourselves agents of righteousness in some way, and we want to take action in defense of God and His kingdom. But dispensing wrath isn't the commission we're given by God.

We're supposed to be people who proclaim the good news of the gospel—through our words and our actions. Yes, the wrath of God is part of that good news; but if the wrath of God is all your news, it's bad news. Because Jesus took the wrath of God upon Himself, making salvation available by God's free grace received through faith.

We're tasked with being ministers of reconciliation (2 Corinthians 5:18), not recompense.

Is it more satisfying for you to deliver news of wrath or reconciliation? Why?

We must stop listening to the voice that tells us to give people what they've got coming to them. That voice comes from our flesh and from the father of lies. It appeals to our self-righteousness. Instead, we must listen to marching orders of the gospel and follow commands like these:

> **"But I tell you, love your enemies and pray for those who persecute you" (Matthew 5:44).**

> **"Just as you want others to do for you, do the same for them" (Luke 6:31).**

> **"Do not judge, and you will not be judged. Do not condemn, and you will not be condemned. Forgive, and you will be forgiven" (Luke 6:37).**

> **"Friends, do not avenge yourselves" (Romans 12:19).**

 According to the *Collins English Dictionary*, to *reconcile* is "to make (oneself or another) no longer opposed; cause to acquiesce in something unpleasant."

 According to the *Collins English Dictionary*, *recompense* is "compensation for loss, injury, etc."

3. *Recast your mission.*

When we focus on the good news of Jesus Christ and remember our proper place when it comes to dishing out justice, we'll maintain a better perspective when personal offenses come up. Charles Spurgeon explained:

> "If a man has injured me, I must forgive him; and if I find him to be faulty, I must love him till he gets better, and if I cannot make him better by ordinary love, I must love him more, even as Christ loved His church and gave Himself for it, 'that He might present it to Himself a glorious church, not having spot or wrinkle, or any such thing.' He did not love her because she was without spot or wrinkle, but to get the spots and wrinkles out of her; He loved her into holiness."[4]

Instead of treating everybody else as if they're beholden to us, what if we treated them like we really want them to "get better" in the grace of God? What if we wanted not the destruction or humiliation of our enemies, but their repentance and restoration and sanctification? Our demeanor, rhetoric, and behavior would change toward them. We would bless them, though they curse us; love them, though they hate us; build them up, though they tear us down; pray for them, though they scheme; and trust God to make things right, though they keep doing wrong.

If we would glorify Christ and not ourselves, this would be our mission. Because that was Christ's mission to us in the face of our hatred of Him.

WRATH ABSORBED

We need to think about these issues. Are we the king of our universe? Do all offenders need to make satisfaction to us? Do we have our own sacrificial system set up—reinstituting something that God has made defunct?

All that carnage; all that blood. Every day unblemished sacrifices were needed—until the dawn of the Son of righteousness. As Jesus spread His arms on the rough beams of the cross, He rose with healing in His wings. When He declared, "It is finished," it really was. And after He rose again—literally, bodily, gloriously—it still was finished.

Centuries of bloodshed ended in an instant when the one, true, spotless Lamb died "once for all."

> **"He doesn't need to offer sacrifices every day, as high priests do—first for their own sins, then for those of the people. He did this once for all when He offered Himself" (Hebrews 7:27).**

 Leading a group? Find extra questions and teaching tools in the leader kit, available for purchase at *threadsmedia.com/sevendailysins.*

That's how serious God is about sin. He wants it vanquished; He wants it killed.

And because you and I are sinners—not just in our deeds but in the basic structure of who we are—we deserve to be sacrificed. God wants our sinful selves vanquished and killed. And He will kill us if He has to.

But our sacrifice won't satisfy. Only a pure offering is acceptable—thus Christ and the cross. Jesus came to satisfy the blood-debt we can't pay. And on Calvary, the wrath of God we deserve was poured on Him. We haven't dodged a bullet, but an eternal flamethrower. Actually, we haven't dodged it so much as our Savior stood in its way.

God leaves no loose ends. When Jesus comes again in wrath for the wicked, He'll bring nothing but the security of His embrace for His children. He hasn't only saved us from judgment but reckoned us holy and undeserving of it!

> **"Much more then, since we have now been declared righteous by His blood, we will be saved through Him from wrath" (Romans 5:9).**

Remember, the cross is the intersection of God's mercy and wrath. The latter Christ absorbs for you, and the former He dispenses to you.

> **"Therefore, no condemnation now exists for those in Christ Jesus . . . "** (Romans 8:1).

Because you're a sinner, you don't know your sinfulness as well as God does in the light of His holiness. But picture yourself at your worst. Think of the worst thing you've ever done—the worst behavior you've ever repeated, the worst pattern or addiction you've engaged in.

Maybe you're in it right now. Maybe you can't seem to get a handle on your pride or your lust or your gluttony or your greed or your envy or your sloth or your wrath. You feel ashamed, broken, demoralized. You feel your sin in your bones.

Before time began, God saw all of this about you. And before you were born, He looked through time, saw you at your worst, and said, "I want that guy." He said, "I'll take that woman."

When this truth settles in, takes root, shakes your foundations, and captures your heart, there's no daily sin that will be deadly for you any longer. You were chosen, loved, bought, and made for freedom. Study the gospel every day and run freely in its power.

THROUGH THE WEEK

> **Pray:** As part of your normal conversations with God this week, ask Him to reveal any areas of your heart that have been impacted by uncontrolled and/or self-centered anger. As you become aware of these areas, repent and ask for healing.

> **Study:** Take some time to study three "prophets of wrath" from the Old Testament. As you read, ask yourself two questions: 1) What caused these prophets to deliver a message of wrath? 2) What reaction did the prophet hope to hear from those who heard his message?

  - Jonah (read the entire Book of Jonah)
  - Ezekiel (read chapters 1-5 in the Book of Ezekiel)
  - Joel (read the entire Book of Joel)

> **Connect:** Commit to making this a week of reconciliation. To start, identify a relationship that was severed or damaged because of wrath—either wrath on your part or the other person's. Pray for healing in that relationship throughout the week, including forgiveness where necessary. When the timing is right, reach out to the other person and ask if you can get together. Make it a goal of that meeting for the two of you to take a positive step toward reconciliation and restoration.

NOTES

END NOTES

SESSION 1

1. C. S. Lewis, *Mere Christianity* (New York: HarperCollins, 2001), 123-124.

2. Thomas Chalmers, "The Expulsive Power of a New Affection," [cited 10 November 2011]. Available from the Internet: *www.monergism.com*.

3. Timothy Keller, *The Reason for God* (New York: Dutton, 2008), 200.

4. Elyse Fitzpatrick and Dennis Johnson, *Counsel from the Cross* (Wheaton, Illinois: Crossway, 2009), 30.

5. J. R. R. Tolkien, *The Silmarillion* (New York: Del Rey, 2001), 6.

6. Trevin Wax, *Counterfeit Gospels* (Chicago: Moody, 2011), 40-41.

SESSION 2

1. Abstract for Peter Johnson's "Pornography Drives Technology: Why Not to Censor the Internet" in *The Federal Communications Law Journal, Vol. 49, No. 1*, 1996. [cited 10 November 2011]. Available from the Internet: *www.mendeley.com*.

2. *http://www.onlinemba.com/blog/stats-on-internet-pornography/*

3. Dallas Willard, "Beyond Pornography: Spiritual Formation Studied in a Particular Case," presented at the Talbot School of Theology's Christian Spirituality and Soul Care conference, September 2008 [cited 10 November 2011]. Available from the Internet: *www.dwillard.org*.

4. Ray Ortlund, "God Gives New Beginnings", sermon preached at Covenant Life Church in Gaithersburg, Maryland, 27 March 2011 [cited 10 November 2011]. Available from the Internet: *http://vimeo.com/21991622*.

5. Albert Barnes, *Notes on the Bible* ,1834 [cited 10 November 2011]. Available from the Internet: *www.sacred-texts.com*.

6. John Piper, "Do You See the Glory of God in the Sun?," sermon preached at Bethlehem Baptist Church in Minneapolis, Minnesota, 26 August 1990, quoted by Justin Taylor, "Why Porno Shops Don't Have Windows,"14 September 2010 [cited 10 November 2011]. Available from the Internet: *www.thegospelcoalition.org*.

7. Maurice Roberts, "O the Depth!" *The Banner of Truth*, July 1990, 2. Quoted in Donald S. Whitney, *Spiritual Disciplines for the Christian Life* (Colorado Springs: NavPress, 1991), 51.

SESSION 3

1. C. S. Lewis, *Mere Christianity* (Westwood, New Jersey: Barbour, n.d.), 82.

2. Billy Graham, *Freedom from the Seven Deadly Sins* (Grand Rapids, Michigan: Zondervan, 1966), 58.

3. Skye Jethani, *The Divine Commodity* (Grand Rapids, Michigan: Zondervan, 2009), 114.

4. "National Obesity Trends," [cited 10 November 2011]. Available from the Internet: *www.cdc.gov.*

5. C. S. Lewis, *The Lion, the Witch, and the Wardrobe* (New York: HarperCollins, 1994), 37.

6. Ibid., location 43.

7. Bruce Marshall, *The World, the Flesh and Father Smith* (Garden City, New York: Image Books, 1957).

SESSION 4

1. Ben Woolsey and Matt Schulz, "Credit card statistics, industry facts, debt statistics," accessed online [cited 10 November 2011]. Available from the Internet: *www.creditcards.com.*

2. *http://www.hulu.com/watch/1389/saturday-night-live-dont-buy-stuff*

3. John Piper, *Don't Waste Your Life: Group Study Edition* (Wheaton, Illinois: Crossway, 2007), 46.

4. "Funny Life Quotes," [cited 10 November 2011}. Available from the Internet: *www.allgreatquotes.com.*

SESSION 5

1. Matt Kruse, "Battling the Envious Soul," sermon delivered at the Acts 29 Northeast Regional in Woburn, Massachusetts, 2 May 2011 [cited 10 November 2011]. Available from the Internet: *www.genesisthejourney.com.*

2. Gary Thomas, *Authentic Faith* (Grand Rapids, Michigan: Zondervan, 2002), 180.

3. J. R. Miller, *Devotional Hours with the Bible, from the Creation to the Crossing of the Red Sea* (London: Hodder and Stoughton, 1908), 25.

4. John T. Mabray, *The Seven Deadly Sins and Spiritual Transformation* (Longwood, Florida: Xulon Press, 2010), 44.

5. Stephen Altrogge, *The Greener Grass Conspiracy* (Wheaton, Illinois: Crossway, 2011), 15-16.

6. Kruse, "Battling the Envious Soul."

SESSION 6

1. Michael Kimmel, *Guyland: The Perilous World Where Boys Become Men* (New York: HarperCollins, 2008), 25.

2. *The "Summa Theologica" of St. Thomas Aquinas, Part 1*, translated by Fathers of the English Dominican Province (London: R.&T. Washbourne, 1912), 432.

3. Karl Barth, *Church Dogmatics, IV.2: The Doctrine of Reconciliation* (London: T&T Clark, 2004), 405.

4. Mark Dever, *The Message of the Old Testament: Promises Made* (Wheaton, Illinois: Crossway, 2006), 513.

5. *Dante, The Divine Comedy, 2: Purgatory*, translated and annotated by Dorothy Sayers (London: Penguin, 1955), 209.

6. Dorothy L. Sayers, *Christian Letters to a Post-Christian World: A Selection of Essays* (Grand Rapids: Eerdmans, 1969), 152.

7. Staci Eastin, *The Organized Heart (Cruciform, 2011)*, quoted by Thabiti Anyabwile, "Some Great Quotes I Enjoyed Today," Pure Church blog, 6 August 2011 [cited 10 November 2011]. Available from the Internet: *www.thegospelcoalition.org*.

8. D. A. Carson, *For the Love of God, Volume 2* (Wheaton, Illinois: Crossway, 1999), 23.

9. Jared C. Wilson, *Gospel Wakefulness* (Wheaton, Illinois: Crossway, 2011), 117.

10. *http://www.reformed.org/documents/heidelberg.html*

SESSION 7

1. Russell Moore, *Tempted and Tried* (Wheaton, Illinois: Crossway, 2011), 18.

2. Dallas Willard, *The Divine Conspiracy* (New York: Harper Collins, 1998), 149.

3. Martin Luther, *"Ephesians 4,22-28" in Church-Postil: Sermons on the Epistles* (New Market, Virginia: New Market Evangelical Lutheran Publishing, 1869), 161.

4. Charles Spurgeon, "Purging Out the Leaven," sermon delivered at The Metropolitan Tabernacle in Newington, U.K., 11 December 1870, reprinted in *The Metropolitan Tabernacle Pulpit, Volume 16* (London: Passmore and Alabaster, 1871), 694.

Threads in no way recommends or endorses these book selections. They are recommendations from the authors and are provided as options for insight and contemplation.

abide

JARED C.
WILSON

INTRODUCTION
THE KINGDOM VERSUS SUBURBIA

"I am the vine; you are the branches. The one who remains in Me and I in him produces much fruit, because you can do nothing without Me" (John 15:5).

Some parts of the Bible sound awesome until I realize I don't understand them. Once I realize I don't understand them, they don't stop being awesome, of course, but my awe is less of the "Wow!" variety and more of the slack-jawed, drooling "Ummm . . ." variety. Ephesians 5:18 is a prime example:

"And don't get drunk with wine, which leads to reckless actions, but be filled with the Spirit."

The "don't get drunk" stuff I totally understand. Tell me not to do something, and I can usually handle it. It's the other part that's confusing. How exactly do you "be filled with the Spirit"? It tells me to do something—which is great—but I have no idea how to accomplish what I'm supposed to do. How do I go about "being filled"? Doesn't the Spirit fill? How do I be something the Spirit does? It sounds as though Paul is telling me to get active about being passive.

And he is.

Though I'm still wrestling with the concept, I'm beginning to realize I'm already quite familiar with the concept of active passivity. And passive activity for that matter.

SUBURBIA
According to the 2000 U.S. Census, 79 percent of Americans live in urban or suburban areas.[1] Most people who will read this Bible study live in what we often simply call "the city" or in a suburb of the city. Every day those of us who live in these areas, particularly in the suburbs and the "nicer" areas of the city, demonstrate with our routines and attitudes that we are experts at actively being filled with the spirit of something. We're shaped by the place and the manner in which we live. By living in a certain manner and in a certain place, we give permission for this shaping to take place, though most of us aren't aware it's happening. That's the same sort of active passivity Paul appealed to in Ephesians 5:18.

If I may be blunt, the suburbs smother the Christian spirit. I know this firsthand because I've spent most of my life in suburban areas. My experience there has taught me that in most cases, both the conscious and subconscious message of the suburbs, in a nutshell, is self-empowerment. Self-enhancement. Self-fulfillment. Self is at the center, and all things serve the self (self-service!). The primary values of suburbia are convenience, abundance, and comfort. In suburbia you can have it all, and you can get it made to order in a super-sized cup with an insulated sleeve.

> WE'RE SHAPED BY THE PLACE AND THE MANNER IN WHICH WE LIVE. BY LIVING IN A CERTAIN MANNER AND IN A CERTAIN PLACE, WE GIVE PERMISSION FOR THIS SHAPING TO TAKE PLACE, THOUGH MOST OF US AREN'T AWARE IT'S HAPPENING.

Whether we realize it or not, the values of suburban culture affect us. They shape us. They slyly dictate how we think, act, and feel. And how we follow Jesus. (Or how we don't follow Jesus, for that matter.) The cultural tide of suburbia is exceedingly difficult to swim against. Almost instinctively, we feel we must have the nice house for our busy family, the nice car to get us to our rewarding job, and the nice neighborhood amenities to make all of life more livable. For followers of Jesus it's a challenge to engage in worship of Him that goes beyond a weekend church service and invades the space and time of the rest of our "real lives."

Most of us make time for God when we feel we have time, doing our best to fit Him in between the paths from house to car, car to work, work to car, and car to house. The problem is that God owns all of life, and worshiping God means we must revolve around Him, rather than the other way around. God shouldn't be confined to a compartment in our schedules. Jesus doesn't abide in His assigned time slot; we abide in Him.

But how do we do that?

RE-FORMATION
Abiding in Him is the process of formation, but that's easier said than done, since most of us have already been formed by the consumer culture we're immersed in. We've adapted quite well to the rhythms of suburbia and we've even stuck a Jesus fish on some of them. To cultivate spiritual formation, then, means to find ways to immerse ourselves in the work of the Spirit—to re-sync our lives to the rhythms of the kingdom of God.

Unfortunately these rhythms are difficult to hear and feel inside the noise of our consumer culture, which is blaringly loud even in the peace of the suburbs.

As the directive to "be filled with the Spirit" indicates, and as Jesus' command to "abide" implies, there must be intentionality and active participation on our part. But the difference between this study and other works on spiritual disciplines is a sense of relief. Many of us grew up in church environments that stressed things like quiet times, service projects, and worship services—which are all good things—in such a way as to create holy homework for the Christian life. The result, at least for me, was not kingdom rhythm but religious burden.

Often missing from my own spiritual formation attempts in the past was the central place of the good news of Jesus' complete and sufficient work. Imagine if Paul had written in Philippians 2:12, "Work out your own salvation with fear and trembling," and stopped there. It's good, solid instruction, but there's not much good news in it. A command like that is sufficient for Christian busywork, and by itself it would be successful at creating more of what it requires. But Paul didn't end the thought there. He didn't just say, "Get to work." He wrote in verse 13, "For it is God who is working in you, enabling you both to will and to act for His good purpose." Now that is good news!

SAILING

Being filled with the Spirit is like sailing. There are roughly 20 to 30 working parts on a sailboat, which means there are always plenty of tasks to accomplish when sailing. You will definitely break a sweat, and you have to stay attentive. But there is one thing you can't control, and it makes all the difference in the world: the wind. You can hoist the sail, but only the wind can push a sailboat through the water.

> OFTEN MISSING FROM MY OWN SPIRITUAL FORMATION ATTEMPTS IN THE PAST WAS THE CENTRAL PLACE OF THE GOOD NEWS OF JESUS' COMPLETE AND SUFFICIENT WORK.

Many approaches to spiritual formation can be compared to getting into a sailboat and then blowing deep breaths into the sail. Consequently we get really tired and have almost nothing to show for our work. The approach of the study you hold in your hands, however, is to help you cultivate the conditions to best live in and enjoy the goodness of the good news. The kingdom of God is at hand. Its rhythms are at work, and they are within your grasp. As you explore these rhythms in *Abide*, I hope your affections for Jesus are renewed, and the life you've desperately needed emerges, bringing God the glory He deserves. A life that follows kingdom rhythms can be lived anywhere in the world, including the suburbs, but it requires an intentional hushing of the consumer clamor so you can focus on the heartbeat of God in the everyday things.

RHYTHM ONE
FEELING SCRIPTURE

I've hesitated to use the word "feel" to describe this vital spiritual rhythm of the kingdom, but after looking for a better word I've come up empty-handed. Don't let the word scare you, though. You don't need to look for "godly goose bumps" or another particular emotional reaction when you read the Bible. If you experience those things, that's great, but in this context "feeling Scripture" means having a deeper familiarity with the message of the Bible, a sense of its big story line, and a comfort with the diversity of its storytellers.

When I sleep some place away from home, I almost always use a night light. I'm not scared of the bogeyman, but I am afraid of injuring myself if I have to suddenly get up because one of my daughters cries or the phone rings. In a dark, unfamiliar place, just getting up to use the bathroom can become a gauntlet of toe-stubbing horrors. But when I'm at home, utter darkness is good. It helps me sleep. And when I have to get up, usually I have no problem finding my way around because I know where everything is, even if I can't see. I have an innate sense of the location of my night stand, the bathroom door, and the dresser. I can maneuver around and through these things in the dark because I'm used to doing so in the light. I never had to practice not running into things; I developed a routine from spending time in my bedroom.

That's what I mean by "feeling Scripture."

Feeling Scripture entails regular inhabitance in the Bible, learning its nooks and crannies, and developing a similar sense of familiarity that we might have with a room in our homes. Jesus liked to use the word "abide" to describe this practically instinctual sense.

But instead of developing that sense, we treat the Bible like an object of utility, not something that is life-giving and active. We read the Bible asking ourselves how we might use it rather than how it might use us.

Thankfully, as we develop our ability to find our way around it, the Bible never gets old or stale. The Bible is a book that teaches us how to read it as we read it.

MESSAGE IN A BOTTLE

A 2007 study by researchers from the Stanford University School of Medicine and the Johns Hopkins School of Public Health tested the brand and logo recognition of preschool-aged children. They discovered that, on this subject, most of these children were geniuses. Two- to six-year-olds could easily identify familiar brand names and packaging, and even if they didn't know the name of the company, they could connect the logo to the product it was most known for. Further, the researchers discovered that even if a hamburger, for instance, did not come from McDonald's, telling some kids that it did resulted in higher satisfaction with the taste than from the kids who knew they weren't eating a McDonald's burger.[2] Not only did these kids know their logos, they bought the message of the logo advertising hook, line, and sinker. Their perception actually changed their tastes.

These kids never had to study product branding. Their parents didn't quiz them with flash cards every night. They hadn't taken any classes on brand marketing. They knew their stuff because kids these days are swimming in marketing messages. Thanks to everything from billboards to book covers, television ads to television shows, radio jingles to Internet pop-ups, nobody has to study product logos to recognize them; they're part of our environment. They *are* our environment.

What are some products you can instinctively identify based on their branding?

Do you think your values have been subliminally shaped by marketing? Why or why not?

The cumulative effect of routine exposure to company branding is just one aspect of the way we're shaped by the daily messages of our consumer culture. The message is practically subliminal. None of us would assent, after all, to a letter in the mail that simply said, "Be more selfish." But that's precisely the message we're hearing—and heeding. Sure, we may laugh at the idea that buying the world a Coca-Cola will teach it to live in perfect harmony, but plenty of us live as though the morning drive through Starbucks or the afternoon trip to the vending machine for a diet soda are what will keep our day on an even keel.

The truth is, the messages of the environments we're most in and the routines we most practice shape our attitudes and behaviors.

They do this in two ways: by bombarding us with their presence and by appealing to our appetites. We all know using Apple computers won't really make us cool, but the Mac vs. PC ads have succeeded like few other advertising campaigns in identifying a desirable culture—hip, witty, smart—with its product. Consequently, Apple gains more market share in the computer world every year. The company has succeeded in pummelling us with their advertising and appealing to our desire to identify with the "cool kids."

The Coca-Cola Company has succeeded in identifying their brand with America itself. Coke products and advertising are seen less as marketing and more as nostalgic vignettes of Americana. We may all laugh at what is truly implied in the slogan "Coke is it!" but Coca-Cola isn't the number-one soft drink in the world because everyone just said "Nah."

If we're going to maintain a vibrant pursuit of Jesus in this culture where a soda (or some other product or experience) is "it," we have to first understand how these ubiquitous messages shape our values. And then we have to learn how to subvert these messages with the more powerful message of the Bible.

Think about some of the items you've purchased in the last year, things like household products, groceries, clothing, magazine subscriptions, books, and memberships to clubs or fitness centers. What promises did they make that you had to believe in order to purchase them?

How might more exposure to the words of Scripture help you find the daily messages you receive from our consumer culture less appealing?

Threads

An advocate of churches and people like you, Threads provides Bible studies and events designed to:

cultivate community We need people we can call when the tire's flat or when we get the promotion. And it's those people—the day-in-day-out people—who we want to walk through life with and learn about God from.

provide depth Kiddie pools are for kids. We're looking to dive in, head first, to all the hard-to-talk-about topics, tough questions, and thought-provoking Scriptures. We think this is a good thing, because we're in process. We're becoming. And who we're becoming isn't shallow.

lift up responsibility We are committed to being responsible—doing the right things like recycling and volunteering. And we're also trying to grow in our understanding of what it means to share the gospel, serve the poor, love our neighbors, tithe, and make wise choices about our time, money, and relationships.

encourage connection We're looking for connection with our church, our community, with somebody who's willing to walk along side us and give us a little advice here and there. We'd like opportunities to pour our lives out for others because we're willing to do that walk-along-side thing for someone else, too. We have a lot to learn from people older and younger than us. From the body of Christ.

We're glad you picked up this study. Please come by and visit us at *threadsmedia.com*.

ALSO FROM THREADS . . .

ABIDE
PRACTICING KINGDOM RHYTHMS IN A CONSUMER CULTURE
BY JARED C. WILSON

Because we're living in the middle of a consumer-driven culture, it's a constant struggle to fit the spiritual disciplines of God—such things as Bible study, fasting, and prayer—in between everything else grappling for our attention. Wilson examines key sections in the Sermon on the Mount and helps us come to see how these practices subvert the rhythms of culture so deeply ingrained in us.

Jared C. Wilson is the author of several books, including Gospel Wakefulness *and* Your Jesus Is Too Safe: Outgrowing a Drive-Thru, Feel-Good Savior. *He is the pastor of Middletown Church in Middletown Springs, Vermont. Visit him online at* jaredcwilson.com.

CREATION UNRAVELED
THE GOSPEL ACCORDING TO GENESIS
BY MATT CARTER AND HALIM SUH

The words we read in Genesis are the same words that provided hope for hungry Israelites in the wilderness, breathed courage into the heart of David, and fed the soul of Jesus Himself during His time on earth. God's promises are as relevant today as they were "in the beginning."

Matt Carter serves as lead pastor of The Austin Stone Community Church in Austin, Texas. He and his wife, Jennifer, have three children.

Halim Suh and his wife, Angela, also have three kids. Halim is an elder and pastor of equipping at The Austin Stone Community Church.

FOLLOW ME
LEARNING ABOUT FAITH, OBEDIENCE, AND BEING MADE HOLY
BY JASON HAYES

When we answer Jesus' call to follow Him, we immediately join in the charge to spread the gospel. But what if we don't know enough? What if we're not ready to change? Or what if our faith isn't strong enough? We're not supposed to have it all figured out—we're supposed to learn as we go, all the while being made holy. That's the process.

Jason Hayes is the young adult ministry specialist for Threads, a speaker, and a church consultant. He is the author of Blemished: How the Message of Malachi Confronts Empty Religion *and the co-author of* Lost and Found: The Younger Unchurched and the Churches that Reach Them. *Jason lives in Nashville with his wife, Carrie, and their three sons.*

FOR FULL DETAILS ON ALL OF THREADS' STUDIES, VISIT *THREADSMEDIA.COM.*